Diana DORS

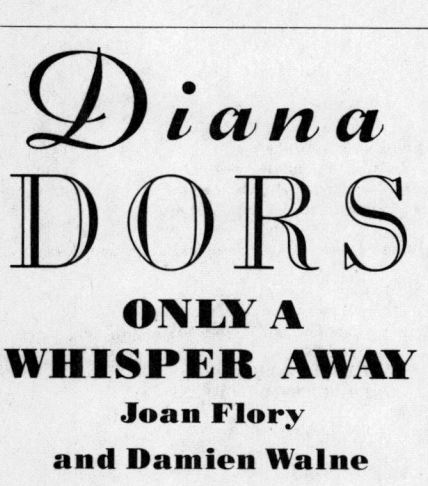

Diana DORS

ONLY A WHISPER AWAY

Joan Flory
and Damien Walne

Lennard Publishing
1987

Lennard Publishing
a division of Lennard Books Ltd
The Old School, Brewhouse Hill
Wheathampstead, Herts AL4 8AN

British Library Cataloguing in Publication Data

Flory, Joan
    Diana Dors : only a whisper away.
    1. Dors, Diana 2. Actors—Great Britain
    —Biography
    I. Title II. Walne, Damien
    791.43'028'0924   PN2598.D67

    ISBN 1-85291-010-0

First published 1987
Copyright © Joan Flory and Damien Walne 1987

Designed by Pocknell & Co
Printed and bound in England by R J Acford, Chichester, Sussex
Typeset by Nuprint Ltd, Harpenden, Herts AL5 4SE

To
Diana and Alan
who opened so many doors

PICTURE CREDITS

Front Cover: Syndication International

Back Cover & Inside: Aquarius Picture Library, London.

Picture Research by David Corkhill

CONTENTS

"LET US SEARCH FOR WHAT SHE FOUND"

Diana Dors, the blonde bombshell of the 'fifties and 'sixties, whose publicity-seeking exploits and extravagant and glamorous life style did much to brighten a rather austere and repressive Britain, needs no introduction. In fact, in the era of the sex-symbol, we were proud to have one who could match the best any other country could offer. She was, as the press said of her, "Britain's answer to Marilyn Monroe".

The Diana behind the image was only allowed to come to the fore when age inevitably began to bury that sylph-like figure underneath more matronly proportions. She became a character actress of considerable talent and then a personality seen frequently on television and heard on the radio. But it was her regular spot on TVam which enchanted millions.

First of all we saw her in the famous 'Slim-in' with the Dors Dozen, openly flaunting those extra stones. In 'Open Dors', an Agony Aunt slot which followed, she answered viewers' problems with a vision and depth that could only have come from living life to the full. Above all, we knew she really cared. She possessed an unforgettable warmth and sincerity in her eyes and a winning smile. Few knew these disguised the agony and trauma of a cancerous tumour which she was trying valiantly and courageously to overcome.

When Diana died we all felt we had lost a friend, a member of the family. The authors went to the Sacred Heart Church in Sunningdale, Berkshire, for her funeral on May 11 1984. During a panegyric given by the officiating priest, Fr Theodore Fontanari, he read one of countless letters and postcards of tribute that had come flooding in. It said:

"I am without faith. I know that something is missing in

my life. Like millions I loved our dear Diana, not as a sex goddess, film star, but as a genuine person who one could feel would befriend you.

"My heart is saddened. Without her lovely being, our world is much poorer. I will now search for what she found."

It was then we knew we had a job to do. It was to find out Diana's secret; to get behind the woman whom millions came to love as the best of British. And so the research for this book began.

The great change in Diana Dors began in 1968 when she met Alan Lake on the set of 'The Inquisitors', a six-part serial for ITV. They immediately fell in love and within six weeks were married. Theirs was a great love which everyone but the family doubted and which Alan Lake wanted recorded for posterity.

This, then, is essentially a love story, telling for the first time the powerful and moving story of their stormy relationship. It is the authors' belief that, contrary to the claims of the sceptics, Alan would have died, had he not taken his own life, of a broken heart.

Our thanks go to so many people who helped us. A special word of gratitude must go to Fr Fontanari, who became an intimate confidant of both Alan and Diana during their last years, and to Ken and Vilma Thursfield, the sister and brother-in-law of Alan Lake, whose family Diana quickly adopted as her own. With their cooperation we were able to peruse the memorabilia of two beloved celebrities.

It has been our honour and privilege to write their definitive biography.

JF & DW

1

"DIANA WILL HAVE EVERYTHING"

"Diana Fluck, what do you think you're doing?"

The teacher's voice had startled the little girl who was staring into space, and she guiltily covered her exercise book with her hands.

"Uncover your book at once. What do you think you're up to?" She rapped the book with her knuckles. "You haven't even started your sums, yet here's the rest of the class almost finished." Then, pointing to some writing down the margin she demanded, "What's all this then?"

"They're film stars, miss."

"Film stars?"

"Yes, miss. They're the names of my favourite film stars."

The schoolmistress shook her head in disbelief. "I don't know about you, Diana. Goodness knows what you'll ever make of yourself. Sums are your worst subject and here you are daydreaming as usual. Goodness knows what your father will say if you don't improve."

The little girl's full lips set into a pout as she thought of her father's stern face.

Although Mr Fluck had got used to seeing his daughter's bad reports it did not stop him from becoming enraged each time the latest was brought home to him.

"There you are, you see," he would say to his wife, who had insisted that their only child should have the best possible education. "What's the point of sending her to a Private School and me having to pay all this money for reports like this? And she still can't do her sums!"

"What does it matter anyway," Mary Fluck would retort, "so long as she can add up the few pounds she's ever likely to earn a week!"

Mrs Fluck was always defending Diana against the wrath of her father. From a very early age the girl had rebelled against his Victorian ways.

Little Diana hated Selwood House School, in the Bath Road, Swindon. She hated its prim and proper Principals, Miss Daisy and Miss Ruth, and she hated lessons. For as far back as she could remember there had been only one thought in her mind: to be a film star.

Diana was taken to see her first film as a toddler and thereafter as often as three times a week. Sitting side by side, mother and daughter were transported into another world where glamorous women wore beautiful gowns and were fêted everywhere they went. Diana wanted to be like that, and to attract men too.

So it was there in the dark cinema that her fantasies and dreams began. She thought life would be like that: big houses, big cars, swimming pools and parties. That is what she wanted, and neither her mother nor her Auntie Kit, her mother's sister, who had cared for Diana after birth during Mary Fluck's illness, told her anything to the contrary.

Her peers, however, were not so encouraging. Jim Masters, a young man who worked under Mr Fluck at the Railway Offices, teased her unmercifully when she made known her celluloid ambitions. Even so, Jim could tell by her firm set chin and utter indifference to his jibes that this vivacious youngster was somehow different to the other little girls.

Young Diana was born with a desire to captivate – especially the opposite sex. She yearned for brothers of her own. How she envied Christine, her best friend at school, who had everything Diana wanted, two elder brothers, and plenty of boyfriends too. And as if that was not enough, Christine had natural platinum blonde hair, whereas Diana's was brown, and, although she had lovely blue eyes, one was lazy and for a time she had to wear a black patch over the good one to make the other function properly. All this added to Diana's discomfort where boys were concerned, and it made her still more determined to become a blonde, alluring film star.

Diana liked to think that her love of boys came from her mother's side, and more particularly from her grandmother, Georgina Dors, who had always let her heart rule her head, only to be let down by the men in her life.

Whoever's traits she inherited, Diana would have claimed them from her mother's side anyway. She was unable to get on with her father, and she sensed his resentment of her more and more as she grew up.

Diana came to learn, mostly from Auntie Kit, that before she arrived, her parents had formed a 'ménage-à-trois' with a young bachelor called Gerry Luck. Having no family commitments, Luck was never short of a penny or two, and neither was Albert Fluck, a capable and conscientious man, who held a good post in the accounts department with the Great Western Railway. This position afforded Mr Fluck an ample semi-detached house on the wide tree-lined Marlborough Road. It was away from 'Railway Village', with its long rows of cream-coloured terraced houses made from local stone, where most employees lived.

All three took their holidays together, sometimes at Georgina Dors's cottage in Wales, but more often at fashionable Weston-Super-Mare, where they rented rooms from a Mrs Bessie Hacker.

They enjoyed the cinema and theatre, attended parties in London, and gave their own 'at homes'. They went dancing too with pretty Mary. Her waist-length hair swinging like a satin curtain, she partnered Albert and Gerry in turn.

'Bert' Fluck, as people came to call him, was respected at work and popular at his club. He was a genuine, down-to-earth man, whose life, moulded by the Army, gave him a great sense of duty and indeed propriety. He was a pianist at one of the local theatres, and was often asked, together with his wife, who sang, to entertain at various social functions. On the nights he worked at the theatre, Gerry would take Mary out somewhere or other, or else they stayed in the house together.

Bert Fluck did not seem to mind – that is, until his wife, who at the age of forty-two had given up all ideas of having a family, suddenly found herself pregnant! The popular 'ménage-à-trois' broke up.

Diana Mary Fluck was born on October 23, 1931, at the Haven Nursing Home, Swindon, Wiltshire. It had been a most difficult birth. While the doctors worked on a mother in danger of dying, the child, who had been struggling for over a week to leave the womb, became black in the face through near suffocation, and was put on one side for dead. But the little scrap had a determination to survive. A nurse noticed, and took her away to another room and tried to revive her. The new-born infant quickly responded.

When the baby was placed in her arms Mary Fluck decided there and then that her Diana was going to have everything that she herself had not. In her youth there had been little alternative for the men but to work on the land, and for the women to go into service in some stately home. This would have been her fate, had she not escaped drudgery by marrying William Padgett and moving to Swindon. Their life together, however, was short-lived, for Padgett was killed in action during the Great War. Mary became one of the country's first post-women, a job which she held in 1919 when she married the dashing young Captain, Albert Edward Sidney Fluck. He had been invalided out of his regiment with a weak heart, having contracted malaria in India.

Diana's life, Mary decided, was going to be different. As well as giving her the best education that was available, Mrs Fluck took her daughter to dancing classes and to elocution lessons, to rid the girl of her West Country accent.

When it came to piano lessons, though, the result was a disaster. Twice Mr Fluck tried to teach her, and when that did not work he placed her with a tutor, but with the same results. Diana would not practise. Mr Fluck gave up and 'washed his hands' of his daughter – not for the first or last time in his life.

Selwood House School, run by the Misses Cockey, Daisy and Ruth, was no doubt one of the better schools around. It did not look pretentious – in fact, little of the old town of Swindon did, with its long lines of monotonous, unambitious grey stone buildings. The school, a converted, rather narrow, three-storey building, with the infant classes on the ground floor, was large enough to accommodate about fifty fee-paying pupils.

The Misses Cockey took a pride in their school and tried to be a cut above the others. Most importantly, they wanted their pupils, both boys and girls, to be 'refined'. To this end such subjects as French, algebra, tennis, plain and fancy needlework, and physical culture, were included in the curriculum. Private lessons in pianoforte and dancing could also be taken for an extra fee.

Diana was not enamoured with life at school. Perhaps she had too much spunk and self-will to allow herself to be moulded into the rather 'genteel' type of young lady Miss Ruth and Miss Daisy had in mind. Rebellion came naturally. She was the instigator of many a practical joke. If someone placed chewing gum in a little girl's hair or a drawing pin on a seat or, worst of all, a beetle or a slug in the French teacher's desk, you could be sure that it was the little Miss from Marlborough Road.

Every day at school was a battle of wits for the irrepressible child. She did all she could to play truant and, with the connivance of her mother, went to the cinema instead. There were so many films she wanted to see. Going to the picture palace on a Saturday afternoon, while Bert Fluck watched Swindon Town play football, was never enough, and she would avoid some classes like the plague. Her pet hates were geography, games, and arithmetic. She tolerated history and enjoyed elocution, drama and reading out loud. The only subject that really interested her was English, and if the writing of film stars' names in the margin of an exercise book had left any doubts in her teachers' minds as to the ambitions of the young Diana, an essay written when she was eight years old and entitled 'What I would like to be when grown up', did not. In it, she wrote of her desire to be a film star, go to Hollywood, have a big house with a cream telephone and a swimming pool. The Misses Daisy and Ruth were not impressed. In fact, nothing Diana did impressed them. Even when she managed to get a mention in the *Swindon Advertiser* for an umpteenth medal awarded for her elocution, their only remark was: "Your conduct in class is the only thing we are interested in".

Winning spoken-word competitions, however, was a far cry from being Betty Grable or Lana Turner. At the seaside with her parents, the child lost no time in aping them, as she paraded up and down the sands in her bathing suit, taking up positions she had seen them adopt in films.

The advent of the Second World War in 1939 was in some respects advantageous for Diana. Her father was called upon to arrange concerts for the troops, and she was frequently used to fill a spot on the bill when an artist failed to put in an appearance. This gave her a chance to sing and dance before a live audience, as her mother had done at concerts for the troops during the First World War.

Diana was thrilled to bits as she went through her repertoire of war songs. Her favourite was 'Ma, I Miss Your Apple Pie'. She would finish by doing a little dance routine, her red tap shoes twinkling around the stage.

The tremendous applause that is always reserved for children not only enhanced her ambitions for film stardom still further but also reassured her that she had got what it takes.

In this little girl's world everything was possible, and she firmly believed that if she wished long and hard enough, it would be.

Her greatest longing was to have her very own swimming pool with warm, clear blue water – to be able to swim whenever she wanted with no worries about boys like Jim Masters pushing her in. And it was to this end that she frequently stood in the rain-water butt in the back garden, eyes closed tight, willing it to turn into a magnificent swimming pool like she had seen in the films.

The nearest Diana got to Hollywood in those days, however, was when the GIs descended on the country. Swindon had its fair share of Americans, much to her delight. Their flamboyant life style, the parties and dances with girls doing the jitterbug, suited Diana right down to the ground.

Behind her father's back, Diana, at twelve-and-a-half, discreetly put highlights in her long hair with a weak solution of peroxide and ammonia. Now, the shouts of the GIs greeted her as she walked down the street:

"Hi there, babe – look, it's Veronica Lake!"

Diana was at first flattered, but gradually began to resent the comparison with Veronica Lake. She wanted to be Diana Fluck, a star in her own right.

Saturday nights soon became dance nights with the GIs. To make herself look older Diana altered her schoolgirl hairstyle, put on her first ever pair of nylon stockings and borrowed a pair of high-heeled shoes. Mary was pleased to go with her to the dances. She had made friends with the camp cook, and the contents of the brown paper bag that went home with her each week made a wonderful boost to the meagre diet afforded by the ration books, and readily appeased Bert!

While Diana danced with the GIs, she was carefully hedging her bets by dating the local boys as well. She sometimes took them to her mother's friend's dancing school to savour the rythmic gyrations of the jitterbug. In particular, she was not at all averse to the company of seventeen-year-old Desmond Morris, who owned a car, and lived in a large house with its own lake containing a small island.

There was just one problem connected with her 'high' living, and that was having to sneak into school undetected by the Americans, whose headquarters happened to be in the Bath Road. With navy-blue beret pulled well forward, and stooped head, Saturday's swinger was once more reduced to a thirteen-year-old schoolgirl.

One day, Miss Knight, the French teacher, asked her to stay behind after school. Despite dating a GI, the teacher received very few invitations to parties held at the base. She was infuriated to be told that one of her pupils attended every one, and from the description it could only be the 'Fluck girl'. Miss Knight told her to curtail her activities with the GIs but Diana, of course, did not. One day at home, after a head-to-head in the classroom, Diana complained that the French teacher had sworn at her. The moment Mrs Fluck heard this, she stormed into the school to complain. Miss Knight denied using bad language, and as a result of a very heated confrontation, Miss Daisy asked Mrs Fluck to withdraw her daughter from Selwood House.

Diana forgot about school when she went on holiday to Weston-Super-Mare. Making use of nature's generous endowments, she entered a beauty competition. While Albert Fluck remained contentedly on the beach reading his paper, Diana and her mother found a pretext to wander off. Donning her modest scarlet and white bathing costume with built-up shoulders, she presented herself at the swimming pool.

The contest, called 'Pin-Up Girl', in which young Miss Fluck appeared, was started by a letter from the secretary to the Director of the Army Welfare Services, asking for photographs of 'bathing beauties' which could be published in *Soldier*, a well-known war magazine. It appeared that the forces were tired of seeing photographs of American film stars, and wanted home-grown girls.

At the final event, show business personality Jack Watson placed Diana third.

"This girl's got something," he said, "I'm damned if I know what it is . . . but she certainly does have it."

Posing by the swimming pool afterwards for a photograph, Diana raised one arm in a wave and rested the other, sporting a wide gold bangle, on the rail of the steps leading into the pool. Her feet, in white court shoes, were placed as perfectly as any film star's.

It was this photograph, displayed in the local *Swindon Advertiser*, which occasioned a modelling offer from the Art Professor at a college opened for the further education of American servicemen. In its wake came invitations to appear in campus stage productions. The first was *A Weekend in Paris*, followed by *Death Takes a Holiday*. She also sang on college radio.

There is little doubt that this time spent at the American college with the gum-chewing GIs marked an important watershed for Diana. The professors had a much wider experience of the world than people she had hitherto met in Swindon. When she mentioned her desire to be a film actress, they could see at once the possibilities in the young woman, and apart from Mary Fluck and Auntie Kit, they were the only others to encourage her.

It was all Diana needed. She went all out to find an acting academy. With details in hand, she approached her father. She knew that he was her biggest obstacle. Albert Fluck had never been happy about his daughter's dreams of 'going on the stage', having, as he did, a good knowledge of the pitfalls of show business. He much preferred that she should take a secretarial course, and later marry some 'decent sort of chap'.

Eventually, they reached a compromise. On the understanding that she study for a teacher's diploma and return to Swindon and teach elocution, Mr Fluck gave Diana leave to go. Thus in September 1945, mother and daughter began travelling to London one day a week to attend private acting classes at the London Academy of Music and Dramatic Art.

During this period, an American photographer at the college, knowing how anxious she was to get into films, arranged for Diana and her mother to visit a film studio. He gave the young hopeful a letter of introduction to a certain Mr Keating, who was directing *This Man is Mine* at a film studio in Islington. The director promised to do all he could to help.

Soon after this her spirits took a tumble. The Americans returned home. Swindon was duller and greyer without them, and life became one great bore. Diana knew that she just had to get to

America to see her friends again and to attain her ambitions of Hollywood stardom. After much wheeling and dealing behind the scenes, Mary Fluck and Auntie Kit finally persuaded her father to let her go to LAMDA (the London Academy of Music and Dramatic Art) as a full-time student.

Diana could hardly contain herself as the new arrangements were made. She was sailing along on a rosy pink cloud, but her father's stern words brought her down to earth with a jolt:

"Failure is unthinkable. It will never happen if you work hard and concentrate on your studies."

2
"THE GIRL MOST LIKELY TO SUCCEED"

A cold wind whipped around the three silent figures standing on the platform at Swindon railway station on a January afternoon in 1946. Diana, though full of excitement, dreams and hopes for the future, could not help feeling sad for her mother. For fourteen years, Mary Fluck's whole existence had centred around her only child, and, although she was happy that her daughter was setting out to do things she herself had never had the opportunity to do, her own life would now be empty.

When the train left, Diana took from her bag her mother's old silver cigarette case. With a lighted cigarette jutting from the corner of her mouth and her beret cocked, she draped herself along the seat of the empty compartment just as Bette Davies might. There was a look of determination on her face that suggested she would do her utmost to prove wrong those scoffers who thought the whole project a foolhardy one and had berated her parents for giving in to such a dangerous ambition.

At Paddington Station, a large hoarding with a picture of Margaret Lockwood, advertising *Drene Shampoo as used by the stars*, further enhanced her resolve:

"One day soon it will be my picture up there advertising Drene!"

Diana arrived at the YWCA with a green suitcase in one hand and a blue ration book in the other.

Next morning, in the company of her new friends, Diana, the youngest student LAMDA had ever had, reported for classes.

She was to study the art of make-up, improvisation, film techniques, Shakespeare, Ibsen and other classics. She was also taught to mime, fence, and fall down dead on the floor. During this period, too, she took and passed her elocution exams with ease.

It was a whole new way of life, and the fourteen-year-old took to it like a fish to water. She lunched each day at a small café in the Earls Court Road, not far from the Academy. The YWCA did not provide midday meals, and for elevenpence Diana was able to eat baked beans on toast and jam roll with custard. The weekly allowance of ten shillings given her by her father went a long way at those prices. Even after her bus fares were paid, there was still sufficient to contribute a little to the student get-togethers, where they sat around at each others' flats, drinking cooking sherry, eating sardine sandwiches and quoting Shakespeare at each other.

On hair-washing nights, she began using a stronger solution of peroxide and ammonia, so that by degrees, instead of having just highlights, her hair became distinctly more blonde.

Diana's most important break at this time was when she acquired an agent. Mr Keating, true to his word, had told the Harbord Agency that here was a young girl likely to succeed in films. Now they contacted Diana with the possibility of a part in the film *Black Narcissus*. Keyed up with excitement, she rushed over to St Martin's Lane to meet Mr Gordon Harbord. He liked the look of her and told her to get down to Pinewood straight away. Thinking it was now just a matter of time before her name would be up in lights, Diana rushed off. To her great horror, she discovered that the part was that of a wind-tanned Nepalese girl.

"Here I was", Diana told a friend at the Academy, "with my first film chance, and the face that I hoped would be my fortune had to look almost like a coal-black mammy!"

In the event, the girl who played the part did not have to look as black as Diana had imagined. It was Jean Simmons, an up-and-coming young actress. As it transpired, the Swindonian had not the slightest chance of success, but the shrewd Mr Harbord was priming her for the battles ahead.

It was a terrible but perhaps necessary blow for someone who had not as yet outgrown her childish notions of an easy road to stardom. However, she wasted no time in getting over her disappointment and, thinking of the money she might have earned, considered other ways to supplement her weekly allowance.

With the help of a newspaper photographer from the *Swindon Advertiser*, Diana obtained an evening job posing as a model for London's Camera Club. When, however, she was asked to pose nude, she consulted her mother, who in turn consulted the head of the house. Bert, already resigned to the fact that Diana would go her own way in life, said it was entirely up to her, and so Diana agreed, tempted by the sizeable fee of one guinea an hour!

When exam time approached, there was precious little time for Diana to find ways of spending her guineas. It was hard graft, for at LAMDA passing exams, be it bronze, silver, or gold medal, was the be-all and end-all of college life; they would determine whether or not a student continued at college. As always, the adjudicator would be a well-known face in the world of films.

Mr Eric L'Epine Smith, a casting director for Warner Brothers, was chosen as the examiner for the first year students' bronze acting medal.

At the end of one of Diana's pieces, scenes from *As You Like It*, *While Parents Sleep*, and *Wuthering Heights*, L'Epine Smith, sitting somewhere up at the back in the darkness, called her to him.

"Have I passed?"

"Not only have you passed, but you've passed with honours". The man beamed at her. "Now listen, I'm casting a film at the moment and I think you'd be absolutely marvellous for a part in it."

"A part!"

"It's only a small part, though."

The student could not care less what the part was, even if it was only one line, so long as she could walk onto a film set.

"There's only one thing," L'Epine Smith continued, "I've seen you act here today and I know you're capable of doing it. But the producer doesn't know your age, which is against you. Now if I go and suggest that a fourteen-year-old girl plays the part of . . . that sort of girl . . . well, he won't agree . . . so just don't go telling him you're only fourteen."

"Nearly fifteen," Diana interjected.

"Well, anyway," said the casting director, "just you say you're seventeen when they audition you."

While Diana prepared for her audition, Bert and Mary Fluck wasted no time in telling everyone in their home town, via the local paper, of their daughter's progress.

> Friends of Mr and Mrs A. E. S. Fluck of 210, Marlborough Road, Swindon, will be pleased to hear of the further success of their daughter, Diana, at the London Academy of Music and Dramatic Art, where she has been studying since September last year.
>
> Following on her awards of bronze and silver medals for elocution, she has now secured the Academy's bronze medal for acting, with honours.

At Wharton Hall studios, Isleworth, the student sailed through her screen test in a kind of haze. Mr L'Epine Smith was delighted at the success of his discovery.

"At a later date," he whispered, "I'll tell him your real age!"

The salary was fixed at £8 a day and the contract for Miss Fluck's first film was drawn up by Gordon Harbord. There was, however, just one problem as far as the agent was concerned, and that was the necessity for a proper stage name. "Fluck" did not exactly epitomise the image of the dazzling star she intended to be. Not only that, when her name went up in lights, Diana said, "What on earth would I do if the letter 'L' went out!"

The Harbord agency suggested Scarlett, after the heroine of *Gone with the Wind*, and Diana had also used the surname Carroll while modelling. But it was her mother, who was in London at the time, who came up trumps:

"Why not use your grandmother's name, Dors?"

Shop at Sly Corner, taken from Edward Percy's stage play of the same name, was produced by George King and starred Oscar Homolka, Muriel Pavlow and Derek Farr. Diana Dors played Mildred, the flashy young girlfriend of Archie, a man blackmailing his former employer. Her scene was a very dramatic one, when the employer comes to offer Archie a small fortune to leave the country for good.

Fortune favours the brave and determined! To be initiated into the nitty-gritty of acting before the end of her first full year as a student, to put theory into practice so early, meant that Diana was indeed lucky. But if the youngster still had any illusions that being an actress was a purely glamorous life, she soon came down to earth with a bump. It was not much fun getting up at 4.30 am, having breakfast by herself, before walking to the station through the pitch black streets of London on a two-hour journey to the studios.

Diana ended her first year at LAMDA successfully. On her return after the summer recess, she received a phone call from her agent.

"Can you dance the jitterbug?" he demanded.

"Can I dance the jitterbug? Why, I'm the best in the country!"

"OK, then, you can earn yourself £10 for a day's work."

Diana needed no second telling and quickly took herself off to Gainsborough Studios, where the film *Holiday Camp*, with Jack Warner, Kathleen Harrison and Flora Robson, was being shot. Towards the finale, in a ballroom scene, Diana, partnered by another young actor, John Blythe, had a solo spot. All she had to do was dance the jitterbug, something she had been doing with the GIs every Saturday night in Swindon's Bradford Hall.

During the exceptionally cold winter of 1947, Diana Dors made it a hat-trick, winning a job at Twickenham Studios in the film *Dancing with Crime*. The star was a promising young actor, Richard Attenborough. Diana was cast as a dance hall hostess. Her salary would be £10 a day, amounting to more than the young actress had ever earned.

On the day filming came to a close, Diana went home to Swindon. The first thing she did was to open the case and display her earnings. She looked on with a great deal of pride as her mother nervously counted the notes – about £150 in all.

"Ridiculous," moaned Mr Fluck, "A fifteen-year-old girl earning more money than I do at my time of life!"

There was a lot of work for Diana to catch up with at the London Academy after her excursion into the world of film-making. In the more insular and unreal environment of LAMDA, obtaining the coveted gold medal and diploma was the culmination of all a student worked for. The time came for less frivolity – with fewer excursions to the cinema, pubs or parties; she only went out nowadays to pick up a guinea or two at the London Camera Club.

She worked assiduously, though all the time waiting for something that had nothing to do with exam results. It seemed like an eternity before *Shop at Sly Corner* was released, and the actress wanted nothing more than to savour that moment when she would see herself on the big screen for the very first time. It happened in April 1947.

"It was an incredible experience," she told her mother.

Mary Fluck had news for her also. The film would be released on May 8 in Swindon and Bert Fluck produced a letter from the Manager of the Savoy with an invitation to the opening night.

The *Swindon Advertiser* went to town. They told their readers that Miss Diana Dors, Swindon's dramatic young artiste, now had her feet firmly established on the path to film fame. Posters appeared everywhere, Diana was overwhelmed with congratulations, and fêted wherever she went. The cinema was packed. The young celebrity, wearing a white evening dress trimmed with silver sequins, and a beaver lamb coat, a gift from her mother, was escorted by her proud father.

After all the 'star' treatment, Diana felt rather like a burst balloon when she returned to London. But not for long. Her agent was on the telephone:

"David Lean is making a film of *Oliver Twist* and they want to test you for the role of Charlotte."

"Isn't that the sluttish maid in the coffin maker's shop?" Her fears were confirmed at the studio where they smeared her face with dirt and dressed her in ragged Dickensian clothes. Diana looked at herself in the mirror and muttered rather forlornly, "Ugh, what a sight. And there's me with my sights set on being Swindon's answer to Betty Grable!"

Events were now moving fast for the young actress. Hardly had she put the phone down to her agent when she was called to pick it up again.

"Diana," said a contented Harbord, "Get down to Pinewood quickly – Rank are testing for possible starlets!"

Film director Sydney Box recognised Diana as she mingled with the other aspiring actresses. He had worked with her on *Holiday Camp* and he remembered that sizzling jitterbug routine. Diana was more than usually confident in her test, and it was with double good news that Diana returned home excitedly the next weekend. She had landed the part in *Oliver Twist* but, more importantly, J. Arthur Rank had offered her a ten-year contract, starting at £10 a week. This would rise annually if they kept their option to retain her services.

Rumours had been rife at college that Diana was going to be awarded the Alexander Korda Cup, given annually to the student of the London Academy of Music and Dramatic Art most likely to succeed on the screen. With her foray into the world of celluloid and a Rank contract that made the other students green, there could be little doubt in anybody's mind that there could only be one recipient.

The presentation was made at the Academy's theatre before a select audience. For publicity purposes, leading film actress Greta Gynt was invited to present the cup. In the reception speech composed for her by her father, who now began associating himself with his daughter's new-found success, Diana promised to do all she could to keep the banner of LAMDA flying high.

No aspiring young actress could have hoped for more than Diana Dors had achieved at the end of her period at LAMDA. The reason for her success was sheer determination. Here was a young lady who knew exactly where she was going.

3
DISILLUSION

J. Arthur Rank had made his millions out of making flour. As a devout Methodist who taught in Sunday School, he felt that his efforts could be enhanced by making religious films. He bought a studio in Iver Heath, Buckinghamshire, called Pinewood.

His interests flowed quite naturally into the secular sphere. Finding the distribution of his films a problem, he solved it by buying a chain of cinemas. As the 'forties ebbed away, he found his new endeavour going from strength to strength, as people crowded into the cinema to forget the horrors of war.

The purpose of the Rank School for young actors, which began in 1946, was to recruit stars. Diana Dors, wildly ambitious and with the talent to match, was in the right place at the right time.

Even though she had completed one-and-a-half years at LAMDA, adding the Alexander Korda Cup to her gold medal, she was soon to find that diplomas meant very little in the hard, competitive world of film making. At the Rank School she had to start again from scratch with other hopefuls, and be groomed to the 'star' image they wished to impose on their contract players. To J. Arthur, deportment, grace, charm, manners and decorum became the order of the day. Instead of learning how to 'fall dead on the stage', Diana found herself walking around balancing books on her head.

There were, however, some consolations. She had a lucrative contract and many more opportunities to add other films to her 'Films I Have Appeared In' list.

In *Good Time Girl* Diana was a delinquent, with Flora Robson explaining the facts of life to her. Then came *It's Not Cricket*, where the comedy team of Basil Radford and Naunton

Wayne ogled her in an amusing scene where she applies for a job in their office. In *The Calendar*, a racing drama, she acted as Hawkins, a prim uniformed maid serving tea to Greta Gynt. And in *My Sister and I* her part was that of a young girl in pigtails delivering a script to star Sally Ann Howes.

Penny and the Pownall Case came next, and it was, of all the films Diana had been in, the one she most hated. For a start, they chopped off her flowing locks, "Simply," she felt, "because the hairdresser could not be bothered to attend to it each day".

Diana's first serious challenge as an actress, though, came from old friend Sydney Box, the director. He chose her to play in a new film which had been inspired by a family portrayed in *Holiday Camp*. In *Here Come The Huggetts*, Mr and Mrs were played as before by Jack Warner and Kathleen Harrison. Starlets Jane Hylton, Susan Shaw and Petula Clark were cast as their daughters.

Diana played the Huggett's flighty niece, a real modern-miss with plenty to say. The follow-up film was *Vote for Huggett*. Pre-publicity was good and she decided to take her mother along to the press review of *Here Come The Huggetts*. Although Mary thoroughly enjoyed the film, the critics did not. That was the first, and last, press screening Diana ever went to.

The next film on the agenda was about cycling clubs and entitled *A Boy, A Girl, and a Bike*, for Gainsborough Studios. Diana was cast as yet another 'bad girl', this time as top supporting actress. Patrick Holt, John McCallum and Honor Blackman were the stars. In the cast too was sixteen-year-old Anthony Newley, who had played the Artful Dodger so wonderfully in *Oliver Twist*.

When she was invited to attend a cocktail party given by the producer, Diana thought she had made it – rubbing shoulders with so many well-known stars. Two weeks later filming started in the beautiful Yorkshire Dales. The sun shone, the setting was idyllic and she was immediately attracted to a tall, handsome blonde cameraman. Diana was in love!

Gil was nineteen, a Norwegian, and the brother of Greta

Gynt. Gradually they began to spend time in each other's company. Evenings after a hot summer's day filming would be spent strolling hand in hand through the still green grass of the Yorkshire Dales. The local village hall also became the venue for parties and dances which were organised to relieve the tensions of filming.

At one of these dances, another young actress, who had been ogling Gil for some time, conveniently fainted right in front of him, in the hope that he would make a fuss of her and escort her home. What was so maddening for Diana was that the ploy worked! She left and went back to her room, furious.

What tormented Diana was that she knew this particular girl had no morals. Because Diana herself was not prepared to go further than petting, she had lost many a boyfriend in the past.

Her mother had warned her repeatedly of the disgrace of an illegitimate baby. Bert, too, pointedly referred on many occasions to men's opinions of women who made themselves 'easy meat', reminding his daughter that every man expected his bride to be a virgin on her wedding night.

A knock on the door quickly brought Diana to her feet. It was Gil. At first she refused to let him in, but changed her mind when he told her that she was the only girl for him. If there was ever a time for her first sortie into sex it was now. And what an anti-climax it all turned out to be! No doubt finding that Diana was a virgin had put the handsome Norwegian off his stroke!

Sex improved, though, and Diana began dreaming of a rose-covered cottage, preferably in the glorious Yorkshire countryside she had come to love, where they could settle down together. She had been completely determined to get to Hollywood, but now all such thoughts vanished, as she turned her complete attention to Gil. As the time approached to shoot the interior scenes at the studios in London, Diana worried only about where they were going to be able to make love at the end of the day. The actress would once more have to report back to the YWCA and the room she shared with three other girls. However, thanks to the salary she was getting from her Rank contract, Diana felt that now was the time to be independent. On her return to London she began looking for a flat. Her parents were horrified when she broke the news to them. But Diana had made her mind up and continued searching. She eventually found an apartment just off the Kings Road in Chelsea. It was one of a large block of flats and consisted of a small living room, bedroom, bathroom and kitchen. For Diana it was heaven. It cost just £5 a week.

While the actress was happy building her love nest, her partner was not. To him a romantic tryst in the Yorkshire Dales was far different from having to settle down. Gone now were those protestations of love. Instead, Gil stunned the poor girl by suggesting they cool it for a while.

Betrayed and broken-hearted, Diana tried to pick up the pieces of a shattered life. Fortunately for her, Anthony Newley had kept in touch and when he said he loved her, Gil was soon forgotten. Her new flat now became an assembly point for out-of-work actors only too pleased to have a place to escape landlords chasing overdue rents. Furthermore, there was always something stronger than tea or coffee to drink.

Diana now got her biggest break. She was offered a leading role in the film *Diamond City*, a story of a boomtown near Kimberley in South Africa in 1870. It marked a watershed in her career, for the gap between star and starlet was like a yawning chasm which only a few, because of their ability, personality and determination, were ever able to bridge. They posed at premières and promoted films at festivals, but only rarely did they appear before the cameras. Most disappeared into oblivion, but not before being compromised in the beds of smooth-talking producers with extravagant promises. Things were different for Diana, because when she first appeared in films she was under sixteen. When Sidney Box knew Diana was in the cast he would circulate a memo to this effect, underlining the word *'jailbait'*. This tended to keep the wolves at bay.

Christmas 1948 arrived, and Diana left London to spend it

with her family. She quickly became bored and anxious to get back to her friends and the dancing school in Hampstead where she was being taught the Can-Can for her new film.

On New Years Eve at the Cross Keys, Chelsea, she met a good-looking, well bred and well groomed young man, who stood out a mile from the other characters around. His name was Michael Caborn-Waterfield. Proud of her casting in *Diamond City*, she naturally tried to impress him, only to be taken aback by his arrogant rejoinder, "I'm off to Hollywood myself!"

Instead of fawning over this shapely, attractive blonde as so many others did, Michael showed only disdain – which merely fascinated Diana. She returned his rebuff, but as the days passed she could not get him out of her mind.

It was at the Cross Keys that they met a second time. Now Michael was charming, and promptly whisked Diana away to the West End. Later she learnt where this extraordinarily handsome nineteen-year-old got his dark swarthy looks – Michael's late father was the Count Del-Colnaghi.

Caborn-Waterfield led a hand-to-mouth existence, though he had high hopes of an inheritance when he reached the age of twenty-one. His dreams of Hollywood were as unrealistic as Diana's had been as a child. He had already tried his hand at many things, including having a go at being a jockey. For the most, though, he earned his living by selling anything he could get hold of, but with his extravagant life style, any money quickly melted away.

With *Diamond City* in the can, Rank was not content to see their contract player 'resting', and sent her off to Worthing to appear with Barbara Murray in *The Cat and the Canary* at the Connaught Theatre. Mrs Fluck accompanied her daughter and the pair enjoyed a couple of weeks at the seaside.

On her return to London, she learnt that Caborn-Waterfield had lost all his money on yet another business venture. No longer able to afford the rent on his lush apartment, he moved in with Diana.

It was not long before Rank were after her again. This time she was sent to play in *Lisette*, a musical comedy which would go on tour around the South Coast.

During rehearsals she found that she was pregnant. The starlet's first reaction was to pull out of the play. Knowing that she and Michael could not afford to have a baby, and the sheer physical illness – she was being sick all the time – made it seem the obvious first step. *Lisette*'s producer, though, would have none of it, and held the girl to contract, threatening to inform her parents and Rank of her pregnancy if she refused. Diana never did discover how he knew about it. She had no alternative but to continue with rehearsals.

Albert and Mary came down to a matinée during the week. Fortunately, Diana was able to conceal her worry and sickness from them when they got together at the end of the performance. After Brighton came Margate, then Eastbourne, where Michael joined her for a while.

Diana's eighteenth birthday on October 23 was memorable. The tour finished, she returned to London and Michael, and she was sick all day long.

They found someone who would terminate the pregnancy, but how to afford the exorbitant sum of £10? Michael eventually managed to borrow on the strength of the inheritance he would receive. The operation was performed on a kitchen table in Battersea.

For Diana the whole thing was a nightmare. It took hours for the operation to end and many months before she recovered physically. Mentally she remained in a bad way for very much longer.

Christmas came, and went, with Diana and the broke Michael struggling to live on her £20 a week from Rank.

One bright spot in the otherwise gloomy winter of 1950 was the release of *Diamond City*. Diana was wild with excitement as she stood in Piccadilly Circus seeing her name in glittering lights for the first time. Was the tide of events turning?

The Rank Studios contracted her out to Elstree, where *Dance Hall* with Bonar Colleano and Petula Clark was filmed. Spring saw her appearing in the play *Man of the World* by H. M. Tennant, which opened at the Shakespeare Memorial Theatre, Stratford-upon-Avon, and then played at the Arts Theatre, Cambridge, and the Lyric Theatre, Hammersmith. It was produced by Kenneth Tynan, a young man fresh from Oxford who had already been earmarked to go a long way. Perhaps because of his direction that Diana received rave notices for her part as a pyjama-top clad young mistress, and she was presented with the 'Actress of the Year Award' by the *Theatre World* magazine. Among other members of the cast was Lionel Jeffries, a young RADA trained actor.

The summer after the play closed saw little work, apart from a 'one-off' called *Born Yesterday*, which only ran for one week at a tiny theatre in Henley-on-Thames. Diana was not worried. She and Michael, together with similarly out-of-work actors, spent their time swimming and sunbathing. The S and F Grill, Piccadilly, an 'in place' for their set at the time, became a regular meeting place. In the meantime, she and Michael dreamed about the inheritance that was coming his way.

The nineteen year old's only real purpose in life at this time was to enjoy it, and she paid no heed whatsoever to her parents' warnings about 'fair-weather friends'. They were right, of course, and those so-called friends quickly vanished the day Diana was told by Rank that all contract artists were being made redundant. The organisation was in debt to the tune of eighteen million pounds. The 'Charm School' was closed.

This was a big blow. It meant that for the first time in her life she was out on her own. No longer cosseted by a contract, Diana found herself in a showbiz world made treacherous by competitiveness, as each actor vied with the other for parts, and ultimately a living.

To help take the sting out of the tail, a small part in the film *Worm's Eye View* came along and netted £275. They planned to keep going on this until Michael's twenty-first birthday and that long-awaited inheritance. The day arrived, but it was to end in misery and disillusionment. As it turned out the Del-Colnaghi business had floundered. Michael inherited £50.

The rent for the flat was soon in arrears. Diana was told to leave. With the coffers empty there was no alternative but to borrow money, write post-dated cheques and live in cheap bed-sits.

Worst of all *Diamond City* had not done very well, and as a result those cherished dreams of Hollywood now seemed a mere chimera.

4

"I'M GOING TO MAKE YOU A STAR"

One afternoon in May 1951, during a break in the filming of *Lady Godiva Rides Again*, Diana went to the S and F Grill in Piccadilly. As she chatted to Jennifer Jayne, another young actress, a man at the next table leant over and asked for a light. Diana was quick to notice that he was handsome. A lock of curly brown hair fell across his forehead, and his smile dazzled.

They had seen each other before and she had played it cool, but when this slim twenty-six-year-old with vivid blue eyes fixed them on hers, she followed him like a lamb to the London Palladium to get tickets for the Danny Kaye Show. Such was his irresistible charm and personality.

"You're Dennis Hamilton, aren't you?"

"That's me." He smiled back. "Come on, my car's over there."

In conversation after the show, they discovered the many things they had in common. They lived in the same street in London, and their father's telephone numbers were identical. Diana's mother and his father shared the same birthdays, as did she and Hamilton. He was seven years older, though, and was born on October 23 1924, to Stanley and Ellen Gittins, in Brymbro in North Wales. The child was registered on November 28 and given the Christian names Dennis Hamlington. Dropping his surname 'Gittins', Dennis changed Hamlington to Hamilton by deed poll.

Diana was to learn a lot about her new companion that evening. Dennis's parents ran a public house in Luton, Bedfordshire, called The Rabbit. At the moment Hamilton was selling water softeners. He had once tried his luck in the acting game, doing 'bit parts', and also as a stand-in for Eric Portman, whom he numbered among his friends.

Hamilton bewitched Diana. Never before had anyone treated her like a lady – and she loved it. The bouquets of flowers which arrived almost daily overwhelmed her.

The fact that Diana's relationship with Caborn-Waterfield was strained helped the new suitor. With money in short supply, they seldom went out any more. Michael was working all hours on his latest project, the buying and distribution of perfume. Ever anxious to make ends meet, he was fair game for shady deals, and one such landed him with a Court summons. The result was a gaol sentence of two weeks. This allowed Hamilton to make his move. He asked her to marry him. At the end of June they became engaged.

When Diana told her parents of the engagement and plans to wed, they approved, even though they had not met her fiancé.

On Monday July 2 1951, just five weeks after they had met, Dennis and Diana presented themselves at Kensington Registry Office. The marriage, however, did not take place, even though Diana had a note with her parents' written consent. The application form for the 'special licence' showed her age as twenty-two. She was in fact only nineteen.

The next day Hamilton made sure they would not be turned down a second time. He had tipped off all the news photographers and reporters that the wedding was at Caxton Hall. The Registrar asked to see the letter of consent, and then refused to marry them. By all accounts, Caborn-Waterfield had got a friend to phone Caxton Hall to say that Diana's parents' signatures were forged, hoping to stop the ceremony. It did not, for Dennis forced the issue by pinning the registrar to the wall of his office and threatening to knock his teeth out!

After the ceremony, the happy couple, in the company of a few friends, went to a small Italian restaurant. As both bride and groom were broke and in debt to the rent man to the tune of £100, the meal was paid for by their guests.

However, Dennis did manage to pay the entrance fee that

evening to the Plaza Cinema, where Danny Kaye, a favourite of theirs, was starring. Back in their apartment, both burst out laughing at the absurdity of it all. They were flat broke and the only thing they had in the world was each other. Even the wedding ring, Dennis admitted, had been purchased with a couple of pounds borrowed from a friend!

How she had settled down to married life with a man she hardly knew, she did not understand. All she did know was that a frothy, raging current of events was sweeping her along.

They moved into an elegant house in Beauchamp Place, Knightsbridge. It was Diana who worried how they were going to pay the rent. As luck would have it, she landed a part in a film *The Last Page*, in which American actor George Brent was starring. The fee she received for her part was £450. With this she covered the post-dated cheques. But when Dennis learnt his wife had given most of that money to Caborn-Waterfield, to enable him to start afresh in France, he went into a rage, and beat her black and blue.

The weeks went by and with no more work in the offing, the inevitable happened; the creditors arrived on the doorstep. It was time for them to move house. With his winning charm Dennis persuaded someone to lend him a car and, once he had loaded up their possessions, drove his wife off to Dunsfold, Surrey, where he had already rented a cheaper house. Diana was dumbfounded. With a career to think of, what, she wondered, would she be doing living in isolation in the country? Perhaps her mother, who visited them, came near to the truth when she whispered to her daughter:

"He wants to get you away from everyone, darling. Out here in the middle of nowhere he'll have you to himself, and as he's so jealous, it suits his purpose well."

By now they were existing on credit from the village shop. Dennis had returned the borrowed car, but obtained another, on credit of course, from the local garage.

In October, *Lady Godiva Rides Again* was released to good all-round reviews. It was a light-hearted romp that took the mickey out of the Beauty Queen business, and the critics found it good fun. Diana, who shone as a hard-boiled beauty queen, hoped that something might follow in its wake, but by the New Year of 1952, nothing had. As the bills mounted up, Diana wondered for just how much longer her husband's patter could keep the wolves at bay. His business selling water softeners was almost on its last legs now. Sales had been poor, due more to the malfunction of the machines than his sales ability. Eventually, Dennis thought up the idea of filling them with sand: that way at least they would stand up during demonstrations!

In February, however, Diana was astonished to find herself in the papers. The American Board of Film Censors had banned *Lady Godiva Rides Again* – all because she wore cami-knickers instead of a slip to cover herself from her breasts to her knees.

Another cause for complaint was Diana's beach-wear. Of all the swimsuited girls in the cast, it just happened that she was the only one wearing a bikini. While the film was under production, the director had made sure that his actress wore two lower pieces, the larger one covering the navel for the American version of the film!

The press, with not a little contempt for American morals, built up the story, with pictures of Diana in the offending cami-knickers displayed over its pages.

This fuss attracted the attention of an American, Robert Lippert, who had worked with her on *The Last Page*. Now he contacted her agent with the intention of building her up into a sex-symbol, just as he had Shelley Winters. The only snag was, he felt he would have a much better chance of doing this if Miss Dors were single. Diana's agent, with an eye to his 10% had the temerity to suggest that she divorce her husband and re-marry him later!

When news eventually filtered through that the American was looking elsewhere, Diana was devastated and burst into tears. Hamilton decided to do all he could to make up for it.

"Dors," he said firmly, "you think you're a has-been before you've ever been anywhere. But I promise you this now. I will build you up to be the biggest star this country has ever known."

"How can you?" sniffed Diana. "I'm finished. No one wants me. I'll end up forgotten.'

"You are going to be the female Errol Flynn", said Hamilton, "always in trouble. I'll see to it that you receive more publicity than he's ever had. I know what we'll do. We'll start by announcing to the press that you have turned down an American contract to stay in England, the country you love. And what's more, we'll say it was a salary of £400 a week!"

Such a strategy was well in keeping with Dennis's flamboyant and outrageous character. The press lapped it up. But although Diana made headlines with this stunt, no work followed in its wake. Dennis suggested a change of agent might help. Diana was reluctant. She had been with the Harbord Agency for five years. Many of her friends, though, had changed agents with some success. The feeling was that it could be beneficial for actor and agent alike. Nevertheless, it was with some regret that she said goodbye to Harbord.

With local tradesmen now pressing for their money, the Hamiltons had no alternative but to move out of Dunsfold. This they did at the dead of night, packing the few possessions they had into the back of their old car.

Esher, their next destination, was nearer London, which raised Diana's spirits. They were dashed again, however, when she had to face another abortion. The question of keeping the baby never entered her husband's head. There was one goal in life for Miss Diana Dors as far as he was concerned, and that was to become a big star. He would allow nothing to get in the way of that. After the abortion, Diana became even more depressed.

Then a proposal of work came in: a live television series with Terry Thomas, called 'How do you view?'

Diana enjoyed the trips to London. She came over very well on the programme, but perhaps too well for some of Britain's first television viewers, who complained about the daringly dressed 'Cuddles', as she was called. Everyone agreed, though, that Diana had a wonderful sense of humour, and made a 'nice little comedienne'. Her fee of £250 paid off the bills which had accumulated at Esher, but it left precious little to live on.

One day, husband and wife went out for a drive in their battered blue Opel, whose big ends were stuffed with sawdust to drown the noise, when a gleaming Rolls Royce passed them with quiet contempt. Dennis saw his wife's covetous eyes follow it.

"We're going to buy a Rolls Royce, Dors. Not tomorrow, next year or some day, but this very day."

"Dennis, you're mad."

"It's the only way to make you a star, the big way, the quick way."

Without more ado, Hamilton changed direction and headed off towards a second-hand car dealer he knew. Once again he put together his smoothest and fastest-talking act. The result, predictably, was that Hamilton acquired a Rolls Royce, vintage 1931, for the price of £365. The old Opel was left as a deposit, and the agreement was for a repayment of fifty shillings a week.

At home Dennis set about cleaning his limousine, having bought some black paint to cover the scratches.

"Dors, he said, peering over the bonnet of the car, "bluff will get you things – modesty won't. From now on, you'll arrive everywhere in a Rolls Royce just like stars should. I'll make it known that at twenty you're the youngest registered owner of a Rolls Royce in the country. That'll amaze the bloody press. I'll tell you now, Dors, this car is going to be your lucky mascot. From here on we'll be in the big time."

Diana, to her amazement, saw Dennis's scheme working almost at once. A man phoned up to offer a job demonstrating a new type of collapsible table at Selfridges. He offered £20 for an hour's work. When they drove up to the store, the department manager was so startled to see Diana getting out of a Rolls Royce that he immediately upped the fee to £50. Little did he realise that the Hamiltons had had to scrape up their last shilling to buy petrol!

The Rolls may also have helped, in no small way, to land her a part in a revue called *Rendezvous*, despite competition from hundreds of girls. The rate for the job was £25 a week. Again, on the strength of the 'Roller' deliberately parked right outside the theatre, Hamilton was able to extort £40.

The revue would open in Brighton before moving to the Comedy Theatre in London. One of the sketches called for her to translate the nursery rhyme 'Miss Muffet' into eight different dialects – from the blarney of Ireland to the excitability of France. This meant continuous practice. At home one spring evening, Diana was going through her paces when Dennis sat up with a jolt.

"What is it, darling?" Diana laid her script on the floor.

"Oh, nothing, nothing."

The actress continued with her lines, unaware of the rare moment of insight experienced by her husband, a moment that would affect her whole life. Hamilton always knew his wife had beauty, elegance, wit and, under her blonde hair, an active intelligent brain. Listening to her range in the Miss Muffet sketch he suddenly realised that she had talent to match. She had everything required to turn her into a big star. With this illumination came the knowledge that he was about to strain every sinew, to fight tooth and nail, for this glorious creature.

With a new-found confidence in the ability of his 'darling Dors', Dennis's first fight was for better billing on the posters. He got it. Not content with that, he had the audacity to change one of her numbers completely. Diana was aghast, and so was the revue's producer, but Dennis had his way. The revised version became a show-stopper in a production that otherwise was mercilessly panned by the critics. In London, it closed after five days – time enough, however, for Diana to make a tremendous impact. The *Evening Standard* theatre reviewer, the influential Kenneth Tynan, was the most glowing in his praise for the performer.

Laurence Olivier was one of many who came backstage to congratulate Diana, and immediately asked if she was interested in a part in the film *The Beggar's Opera*.

Various plays were in the offing too, and a summer season at Blackpool for £100 a week. There was also an idea put to the young woman by a variety agent, who guaranteed £135 per week for each week of the year to perform a twenty-minute act around the music halls.

Diana was indignant.

"I'm an actress. That's what I've trained for, and that's what I want!"

"OK," smiled the agent, "it's all very well now. You may have conquered London. But there will come a time when this whole show and your success will be forgotten. You have to decide whether you're in this business for the money or the glory. And you can't eat press cuttings."

Dennis opted for the Blackpool season with Bebe Daniels and Ben Lyon in 'Life with the Lyons'. Diana found herself a step closer to the cabaret she so much wanted to avoid.

Nevertheless she worked hard at Blackpool. She had to do two shows a night for twelve weeks. Diana was quick to dismiss rumours of Denis's unfaithfulness, especially as he began to dazzle her with his new-found knowledge of percentages, fees and other showbiz know-how.

"You know, Dors," he would repeat, "your £100 a week is peanuts. Put an act together. Artists are earning £1,500 a week for variety!"

A big influence on Hamilton at this time was Joe Collins, a well-known show-business agent, and father of Joan and Jackie Collins.

"Talent's not everything," he told Dennis. "If Diana has a personality she will last." And, echoing what Dennis had always thought, "*Diana must behave as a big star.*"

With the Blackpool season over, there was enough money to move back into London. The Hamiltons rented a small cottage in Chelsea. Almost immediately Diana netted another film, *The Great Game*, in which her husband was persuaded to play a small part as her boyfriend. Although producers were continually trying to get him into films, Dennis wanted fame not for himself, but for his wife.

The Hamiltons' luck was well and truly in. Impressario Jack Hylton, who had approached Diana at the Comedy Theatre, now came back with another offer of a part in *Remains to be Seen*, the Broadway hit, which he planned to open in the West End. The fee was £175, a huge sum for a straight play.

"It is a thriller," he told Diana, "a 'whodunit'. But it's a 'funny' murder all the way through. You'll be just ideal."

To the amazement of the theatre world and the stupefaction of the cast, the play, which opened at Her Majesty's Theatre in the Haymarket, was so slated by the critics that it was forced to close within a week of its opening.

Diana had been looking forward to a good run in the West End, perhaps even emulating the seven-month Broadway run the show had. This she felt would make up for her disappointment with *Rendezvous*. She had already planned out the £175 a week pay which would put her financial embarrassments behind her. That night, even the thick-skinned Dennis was in tears.

"Oh God, darling," he put his arms round her. "You've worked so hard and deserve so much better than this."

The only consolation was that his wife had received great notices. As actor friend Bonar Colleano quipped, "When is Diana Dors ever going to flop in a success?"

5

TREADING THE BOARDS

In spite of her two West End failures, Diana was chosen in December 1952 as the first sound radio Pin-Up Girl. She would have broadcast regularly on the 'light programme' had not Hamilton objected to her not receiving top billing! The truth was that his mind was set elsewhere. Nothing, he felt, but Variety would land him the cash he envisaged.

Dennis once again began trying to persuade Diana to put a Music Hall act together. Diana would have none of it. This caused many violent tantrums and she often rued the day she had met him.

Not a year had passed since her personal success in *Rendezvous*, and already the revue and its star had been forgotten. Swallowing her pride, Diana accompanied Dennis to watch different cabaret acts, so one could be worked out for her. And when an agent wishing to cash in on her film status offered her a five-week booking at the largest variety theatres around the country, Dennis jumped at the suggestion. Her first excursion into Cabaret was to be the Empire, Glasgow, the graveyard of many an artist!

With a heavy heart Diana began putting an act together. It was largely a burlesque of film personalities. She caricatured Ava Gardner, impersonated Rose Murphy and made fun of Rita Hayworth.

When it was time to go to Glasgow, they travelled by overnight train, and then by taxi to the theatre. Outside was a queue of people, four deep, stretching round the block.

"My God!" the agent shouted as they drew up at the stage door, "I thought you might be a draw, but I never imagined anything as fabulous as this,"

An equally elated Diana greeted the man on the stage door.

"What a wonderful queue out there. We should do good business this week with that amount of customers."

"Och," said the man in a thick Scottish brogue, "That's not for you. It's for the Sunday concert next week. It's a great bill — full of Scottish artists!"

Deflated but not daunted, the blonde swung her hips even more as she made her way into the theatre.

"I'll show ye to your room," the man offered. "It's the Star one, ye know. We've had all the biggest ones here: Danny Kaye, Judy Garland, Frankie Lane..."

The stage door keeper droned on, reeling off stars of such magnitude that even before reaching the dressing room, Diana's knees had turned to jelly. She wondered what on earth she was doing in Glasgow, let alone appearing at the great Empire Theatre, doing something that she had never attempted in her life before.

"Have you got a lighting plot?" was the first question the stage manager asked the top of the bill.

"Er, um... well, you know this theatre better than I do. I'll leave it to you."

Diana spoke nonchalantly, wishing she was safely ensconced in her mother's home in Swindon!

That evening, while Dennis chewed his fingernails, Diana made her first entrance onto the music hall stage — with a great fanfare of music she began her specially composed 'show stopper'. Nothing.

From then on, every joke, every line of each song, received nothing but total silence. And there was only a trickle of applause when her act came to an end. Diana's twenty-five-minute spot had seemed an eternity. A less redoubtable person would have found a way to leave the stage a lot sooner.

"My God," gasped Diana as she fell into her husband's arms, "I'm a complete wreck. I died a thousand deaths out there."

"Nonsense," said the manager standing in the wings

beside them. "You went very well. At least they didn't throw things."

The critics next day were quick to explain the artiste's first night flop:

'The reason lay in the faintly nasty, singularly witless number which Miss Dors had specially written for her opening. She would have done so much better merely to have come on and given us a bibful of old sentimental tunes.

For the gal can sing, she has presence and aplomb, and she could have charm, too, if they put different lyrics in her mouth.'

Diana took it all on the chin, and the coterie around her went immediately to work trying to put a better act together. They changed words, jokes, songs and even the opening number. Her spot was cut from twenty-five to fifteen minutes. But it was too much to expect matters to improve in such a short time. The valiant Miss Dors had to relive her nightmare for the remainder of the week.

For this, she received £250, more than she had ever earned for a week's work. The sight of the cash cheered Hamilton up.

"This is the game, Dors. To hell with all that acting rubbish; it's for the birds! In Variety we can make real money!"

With the pound sign flashing above his head, Dennis then wheeled her off to Brighton, Birmingham, Portsmouth and Hull, which completed the five-week tour. Then he changed their agent and, together with the new one, worked out a different routine. As always, Diana had no say in the matter. Soon she was hoofing it again in music halls around the country. This time, they played more familiar territory: May 1953 saw her in Swindon.

To take such a risk in one's own home town meant that Diana had got over her Glasgow embarrassment and found new confidence in her own ability as a Cabaret artiste. She also had the advantage of a more professional back-up team, and this showed.

Luton audiences had been appreciative, and the Empire Theatre, Swindon, enjoyed one of its biggest ever houses for a Monday night.

"My appearance here is quite a family affair," she told reporters. "My father was pianist here for four years and my mother often played on this stage in amateur musical shows."

At the end of the performance one reviewer wrote:

> 'Miss Dors's act is a skilful blend of showmanship, short, cleverly written and constructed and tailored to her personality. It is not original but it shows that Miss Dors has versatility of talent, and knows how to make the most of good material. She should go far in the entertainment business.'

With twice-nightly performances and increased weekly takings, Dennis began eyeing a most attractive house which had been put on the market, in Burnstall Lane, Chelsea, not far from their present cottage.

"Property is the thing, Dors. It's bad economy to throw away money on rent. We have to consolidate for the future!"

Using a large part of his wife's earnings he secured the house on a mortgage, and then arranged to send her off to other music halls. With the prospect of more money, and £1,000 for making a film with Northern comedian, Frank Randall, Dennis began home improvements.

With a view to keeping his wife in the headlines, Dennis also had her pose for daring pin-up pictures in the studio extension of their new home. It had occurred to him for some time now that England should have its own equivalent to Marilyn Monroe. By 1953, thanks to her successes in *Gentlemen Prefer Blondes* and *How to Marry a Millionaire*, Marilyn was a well established sex-symbol, and other countries were coming forward with their own equivalents. Diana would be England's answer.

She herself was not keen on the idea, even though she had all the necessary attributes, believing that it might jeopardise her aspirations to be taken seriously as an actress. This objection was immediately overruled. Jumping on the 3D bandwagon, the latest craze, Dennis worked out a series of poses to be taken of Diana, amid exotic backgrounds. The pictures were published in book form, and called *Diana Dors in 3D*. It came complete with a pair of red and green spectacles for viewing.

Hamilton was creating the image he wanted. Diana had stepped one stage ahead of the pack and was destined to be Britain's sex-symbol. Brigitte Bardot had claimed the crown for herself in France, Gina Lollobrigida in Italy, as Europe, like America before it, shrugged off the austerity and sexual repressiveness of the post-war years. Diana's sex-symbol image, flaunted so deliberately in 3D and in her contrived, extravagant life style, were carefully manufactured to meet this need.

6

BRITAIN'S BIGGEST STAR

When the chance to play a straight role in the film *The Weak and the Wicked* came along in August 1953, Diana grabbed it with both hands. She was determined to show the public she was more than a 'B' movie actress, and that she had more to offer than a figure for a bikini. The star of the film was Glynis Johns. Diana was cast as her friend in prison.

The film was based on the book *Who Lie in Gaol*, by Joan Henry, who had herself been gaoled. During the filming, Ms Henry told Diana that she was writing another story, this time with the grim theme of a woman's last days in the death cell for murder, and that Diana was being considered for the part.

At the end of the film and between variety engagements, Diana was asked to do a radio series, 'Calling all Forces'. Bob Monkhouse and Dennis Goodwin were engaged as script writers for the current series of what had proved a popular programme. Again, it was welcome break for Diana. She particularly enjoyed Sundays at the Garrick Theatre, where the show was broadcast. It was then that Bob Monkhouse, for whom she had developed a liking, would appear. Inevitably Dennis got to hear about it, and his jealousy knew no bounds. He wrongly accused her of being unfaithful and then proceeded to smash up most of the contents of their Chelsea home.

At Christmas, Diana found herself teaming up with Wee Georgie Wood in the pantomime *Aladdin*, at Southampton. Unable to see any future for herself and Bob Monkhouse, Diana, to her regret, had to cool the attachment. Her husband celebrated by hoaxing Wee Georgie Wood and other members of the cast. On one occasion he put two 56 lb lead weights in Widow Twankey's laundry baskets; Wee Georgie Wood could hardly move them around the stage.

In February 1954, *The Weak and the Wicked* was released.
One reviewer wrote:

>'Diana Dors, Britain's great white-haired hope, in her
new film *The Weak and the Wicked*, made me cry; real tears, mind
you. She did it by sheer acting ability as a gaol chick pining for
her lover. It was such a refreshing change from the parts she
has been playing for the past seven years.'

Despite the excellent reviews no more films were coming
Diana's way. What worried her most was what some producers
told her when she went touting for business: "You are box office
poison, Miss Dors – and all this saucy publicity you are getting
won't do you any good."

When *Aladdin* ended, Hamilton took his wife on a short
holiday, and then it was back to the song, dance and patter of
Variety, which continued to earn her £300 a week. He reasoned
correctly that with the growth of television, music halls were on
their last legs. One had to cash in before it was too late. By now,
Diana's act was perfectly tailored, and so were her gowns. In
particular, the one she wore on stage at the Chelsea Palace
consisted of 257,000 cerise sequins all sewn in place by hand and
covering the whole garment. Pictures of her in this dress
proliferated, and ensured she would be kept in demand.

Though busy with work, Diana still felt that time was
passing her by. Professionally, very little demand was being made
on her abilities, and on the home front, what used to amuse her
about life with Dennis now palled. His sense of humour and
endless practical jokes no longer appealed, and they had little else
in common. Monkhouse's company had only emphasised this.
Also, her husband's moods would change unpredictably.
Sometimes he would open all the windows in the house when his
wife and guests were freezing, or knock over furniture complaining
he had never seen it.

But as is the way with show business, a purple patch is ever
likely to follow a black one. By far her biggest break as an actress

came soon after in August 1954, and from an unexpected source. A lead was being sought for Wolf Mankowitz's *A Kid for Two Farthings*, directed by one of the doyens of the British cinema, Sir Carol Reed.

It had always been the Swindon girl's ambition to work for a top director. Young or not, she fully realised how important and influential a good director could be in one's career. Now Miss Dors had a chance of working with one of Britain's greatest. Sir Carol, after six years as stage adapter for Edgar Wallace, had shot to pre-eminence in 1948 by bringing Graham Greene's short story *The Fallen Idol* so convincingly to life on the screen; he had then followed this up the next year by directing the internationally successful *The Third Man*, also from a story by Graham Greene.

Diana Dors had always wanted to work for him, and now she was going to do her damnedest to get this role. Despite some producers having labelled her box-office poison, *The Weak and the Wicked* astounded everyone by being a major hit. The blonde, buoyed up with optimism and a package of good reviews, joined a line of young actresses being interviewed for the part in *A Kid for Two Farthings*. She did not care about the apparent gulf that existed between her film exploits and his – she, the glamour symbol, and he, the leading and most thoughtful of British directors. She just felt that she had a chance and hoped that this man, who obviously knew about her most flaunted assets, would realise that she could act too.

The interview and audition went well for Diana. Like the string of other young hopefuls, she would have to wait to know the outcome. At this time all sorts of doubts assailed her. There was strong competition and, like all actresses, she had lost out on auditions many times before. Yet she had a gut feeling she was in on the reckoning.

After ten nailbiting days, news came through. Diana had got the part.

"I've seen a lot of her films," said Sir Carol, when interviewed about what was seen as very controversial casting, "and I thought she was right for the part. I ran them through again, and I was sure. I think she has a fine sense of comedy, and I also wanted a girl who could act. Diana is a nice little actress."

The film is about a small boy who buys a baby goat with one crumpled horn because he thinks it is a unicorn and unicorns can make wishes come true. The boy's wishes, though, are simple. He wants a steam press for an old tailor (David Kossof) who looks after him, and his friend (Joe Robinson) to win his next wrestling match so that he can afford to buy an engagement ring for his girl, played by Diana Dors.

Diana's fee for *A Kid for Two Farthings* was £1,700, and with money piling up from Cabaret the restless Hamilton sought a move back into the country and to a much more lavish home than their last.

They chose the Royal Borough of Berkshire, already a *pied-à-terre* for the stars of showbusiness. A luxurious property appeared on the market at Bray, a stone's throw from the film studios of that name and quite near to the other studios at Pinewood, Shepperton and Nettlefold. Just ideal for the 'star' who was going places!

Her landing of the part in the Carol Reed film made many in the industry do a double-take on Diana. Among these were former employers, J. Arthur Rank, who renewed their interest in Hamilton's 'commodity' by offering Diana a seven-year contract worth £100,000. Hamilton, unusually for him, felt a bit out of his depth. He immediately enlisted the help of a top class agent to deal with his wife's affairs. They came no higher than Mr Al Parker, who had most of Britain's leading actors on his books, and had the knack of getting the best deals. The first advice he gave was to turn down the contract, fully convinced Diana would fare much better as a one-woman concern than as a contract artist.

Diana, too, saw the logic of this. She reasoned that had not her first ten-year contract with Rank been terminated, it is most unlikely that she would soon be living in this opulent house.

Brook Cottage, their home in Bray, was situated in 2½

acres of garden which swept down to the river's edge. Hamilton quickly revamped the ten-roomed property. He added three bathrooms, one with a marble sunken bath big enough to swim in, and a private cinema with leopard-skin chairs. Part of the large boathouse he turned into a bar; the remainder he filled with a 20 ft motor launch. In the garden there was an aviary filled with 20 tropical love birds, budgerigars, cockatoos and parakeets.

Replacing the £360 battered old Rolls Royce, which had been very discreetly disposed of, was a new Cadillac with the initials DD embossed in silver on the door – a present to Diana from her husband. When he presented his wife with this brand new powder-blue limousine, she quipped, "Blue is a wonderful colour for blondes: even our lawn mower is blue."

The problem was that she still could not drive. When she failed her test the second time round, there was a posse of photographers present when she stepped rather forlornly out of her Cadillac.

"They don't expect blondes to be able to drive straight, darling," she called out to one of them. "Next time I'll go in heavy disguise and drive a Morris Minor!"

"What did he fail you on then, Diana?" the man shouted back.

"I failed because I didn't use the mirror. I ask you, darling, fancy me, a film star, forgetting to look in the mirror!"

A much greater embarrassment was suffered when the police in Halifax brought action against the book *Diana Dors in 3D*, which was now selling like hot cakes. They wanted it banned from public sale on the grounds that it was obscene. The controversy naturally made good copy, and headlines such as "Halifax Magistrates say Diana Dors is Obscene" appeared everywhere: not at all becoming of Carol Reed's leading lady. It upset Diana greatly.

After a month of deliberation, Halifax magistrates decided that *Diana Dors in 3D* was not obscene and dismissed the police's application to destroy the book.

The filming of *A Kid for Two Farthings* ended in November. It had been a very useful experience for Diana to work with a polished director. Having a major part ensured that she was almost always under the supervision of Mr Reed.

"I've learned a lot – I'd a lot to learn", admitted Diana. "And I play a nice girl for a change. Hope I'm convincing!"

For her next film, *As Long as you're Happy*, in which she made a guest appearance, she was paid £200 a day, her highest ever rate. Not to be outdone altogether, Rank reached a compromise agreement with Hamilton on the services of the blonde who was now becoming the hottest property in the business. So as to keep her options open, he agreed to one film a year for five years. For her first film, *Value for Money*, Diana received a record £8,000, in keeping with her newly acclaimed 'star' status.

If this was now the going rate for a 'Dors' movie, then those who marvelled at her turning down a Rank seven-year contract worth £100,000 could now marvel at her shrewdness or, more correctly, her agent's. On an annual basis of three films a year, it was not hard to work out that she would receive in four years what Rank offered her in seven.

The acquisition of a 24 ft Delahaye sports car, the only one of its kind in the world, was yet another gauge of the Hamilton's growing prosperity. At a cost of £6,500 it took its place alongside the Dors' Cadillac. On the car's dashboard were twenty-one gold-plated controls, and a crystal and gold-plated steering wheel. The coachwork was in powder-blue to match the Cadillac – and the lawn mower! The car did 150 miles an hour at six miles to the gallon.

When she was first led to inspect the wonder-monster, Diana pointed to the dashboard and the door handles, and then began rubbing them with a handkerchief.

"What are you doing, Dors?" her husband demanded.

"I'm trying to clean off the rust."

"What do you mean rust? Don't be silly – that's gold!"

The producer of *Value for Money*, Sergie Nolbandov, was near to rebellion when Diana was foisted upon him. He was one of the school of producers, who considered her a liability because of her notorious publicity. Only after interviewing her at the request of Ken Annakin did he change his mind.

Ken Annakin, who had known Diana since her early film days, was a great supporter: "Losing that starlet contract with Rank was good for her," he said. "Before, she was just like any other starlet. Now, she is a real professional. She is never late, never minds working overtime, never arrives with spoilt make-up or dis-arranged hair."

Should Sidney Box have met Nolbandov, he would have assured him in similar fashion about the role she was called upon to play: "Diana hasn't the horsey looks that many British women have. Like American girls, she has the knack of displaying sex appeal on the screen."

Diana was game for anything that should be asked of her on the set, and at the end of a hard day's work, when most actresses are worn out, the production team of *Value for Money* found that she was still willing to work. Everyone came to admire and respect her. She was very different from the silly, giggly girl projected in her publicity. She was the professional Annakin said she would be, expecting no favours and enjoying a matey relationship with the unit. Getting ready for the film's most revealing shot, she turned to the cameramen and said, "OK boys, take a good look now and let's get on with it!"

Diana never minded peeling down to silk and lace. She was well aware she had a good figure and was not at all self-conscious about showing it off.

"You should have seen me yesterday," she bubbled next day to her guests at the studio, "I was starkers." No doubt appearing before London's Camera Club had rid her of any modesty she may otherwise have had.

It was in April 1955, while filming *An Alligator Named Daisy* at Pinewood studios, that Diana suffered her biggest personal setback. Her 65-year-old mother died. Three weeks earlier, Mary Fluck had gone to London for what was expected to be a minor operation. It was found to be serious. She made a good recovery, however, and was up and about again and preparing to go home. Then quite suddenly, she collapsed and died. The star was devastated when the news was broken to her and the studio sent her home. Filming was postponed until the following week.

What grieved Diana so much was that her new-found fame and fortune could not be shared with the one who had introduced her to the cinema and, indeed, had given her every opportunity to succeed.

Mary Fluck had hoped her child might have achieved some of the cultural acclaim of such actresses as Margaret Lockwood, Jean Kent or Vivienne Leigh. More often than not, what she had to read in the papers was far from it. Yet when Diana sat and thought about it, she realised that *The Weak and the Wicked had* brought her some dramatic acclaim, which delighted her mother, as had becoming Carol Reed's leading lady. Also, before her death, Mary Fluck had been aware of the recently arranged Rank contract. This positive thinking helped Diana in her grief and, after the funeral, she flung herself back into work.

A Kid for Two Farthings was previewed in May 1955 to wonderful notices. Harold Conway in the *Daily Sketch* wrote:

> The day – I thought – that a film director could cut Diana Dors down to size, make her forget all about screen sex and the body beautiful – that day I thought, she would be a very nice actress indeed.
>
> Yesterday I saw the preview of a film in which the miracle has happened!

As a Rank contract player, Miss Dors was obliged to attend the Venice Film Festival. It was the first excursion of this nature that Rank had attempted. The object was to give the company a boost and help sell British films on foreign markets.

A gleaming Viscount aeroplane, chartered from BEA, was

boarded at Heathrow airport by John Davis, the Managing Director of Rank, and his team of stars. Among these were Jack Hawkins, Belinda Lee, John Gregson, Donald Sinden, James Robertson Justice and Eunice Gayson. Backing them up was a team of publicity men, gossip columnists and a frame of photographers.

When they arrived at Treviso Airport, a fleet of limousines took them to the water's edge. They went down the Grand Canal in motor boats, across the lagoon where the flagship of the Royal Navy's Mediterranean fleet, HMS Sheffield, was anchored, to the long, narrow island of the Venetian Lido. Here, where the Union Jack fluttered on countless flagpoles, was their hotel: the plush Excelsior, the focal point of the festival.

The only star not to accompany them by aeroplane was Diana Dors. She travelled all the way to Venice by gleaming Cadillac, partly to be different, but partly because of her husband's fear of flying. They were to make full use of the limousine. During a week of film shows, parties and receptions, and with every balcony, loggia and window crammed with spectators, Diana was photographed in her tight-fitting dresses getting in and out of her sumptuous car.

When the press first heard that Diana Dors had been asked to go to Venice, they were anxious to know what gimmick she had tucked up her sleeve. The star, accepting that being saucy was a tag she could not live down, decided to give the public their money's worth.

She had always wanted a mink coat, which her husband continuously refused to let her have. If she could not have a mink coat, she would have a mink something else – and put it to good use. The blonde with the gorgeous figure caused quite a sensation in pious Italy – as she was propelled down the Grand Canal in a gondola, in a mink bikini! Photographers vying for a picture fell one by one into the canal, all for the sake of their art! Pictures of Diana so clad circulated the world the next day....

From mink bikinis and powder-blue Cadillacs to

Government regulation blue calico prison uniform was quite a bizarre transformation for Diana. So was the grandiose renaissance background of Venice, to a plain four-walled cell at Elstree Studios. The long awaited role, promised her since *The Weak and the Wicked*, materialised later in 1955. J. Lee Thomson, was directing the film, based on Joan Henry's book about a condemned woman murderess, called *Yield to the Night*. Diana had beaten off such actresses as Vivienne Leigh, Margaret Leighton and Ingrid Bergman for the part.

The film, as the book before it, was a powerful plea against capital punishment and had the added poignancy of being made soon after the execution of Ruth Ellis. Miss Dors played Mary Hilton, infatuated with a handsome night-club pianist. He leaves her for Lucy, a wealthy society woman. Lucy deserts him and he commits suicide. Mary decides Lucy is responsible for his death and appoints herself executioner. In the film she awaits her own execution in the condemned cell at Holloway prison. Devoid of make-up, and blonde locks scraped back from her forehead, Diana shrieks at women warders.

Hamilton, meanwhile, scoured the country looking for more property to invest in. One day he dragged his unfortunate wife off the set to Maidenhead to look over his intended purchase: a rambling Victorian mansion. It stood on several acres of land that edged the Thames by Boulter's Lock. There were twenty-three bedrooms, two lodges, a stable, tennis and squash courts, and, what by now was a necessity for Diana, a covered swimming pool. This was Roman in style. The price was just £12,000, which Hamilton saw as a bargain not to be missed, particularly as his wife was getting £8,000 of that sum just for one film with Rank.

While Dennis was converting his new purchase into a sumptuous 20th century extravaganza and feeding the pool with fresh clear water syphoned from deep beneath the Thames, Diana continued with *Yield to the Night*. She was very happy with the role and her performance. She had waited ten years for a part that would tax her and ultimately satisfy her ability as an actress. She lived Mary Hilton every single day.

One of the highlights of 1955 took place on November 7 when she was presented to the Queen at the Royal Command Performance. In answer to the Queen's "You're making a film at the moment, aren't you, something sinister, isn't it?" Diana was able to tell Her Majesty about *Yield to the Night*.

It was a very proud moment for the young star, a moment she would have loved to have savoured with her mother, as Auntie Kit, who was now looking after Bert Fluck, mentioned in a congratulatory letter.

1955 ended on another high note for Diana Dors. In the British cinema popularity poll she was voted Britain's top female star. Dennis's prophecy and promise to make her Britain's biggest star had come true!

Somewhat surprisingly, Diana had to wait some time before she was offered another part, and that was only in a Norman Wisdom comedy for Rank. Hamilton turned it down as hardly a worthy follow-up to the prison drama. He did, however, accept an offer for his wife to appear in a Bob Hope television spectacular. It was for American viewers, although shot in England, and Bob wanted Britain's sex-symbol to be with him.

As the young actress waited eagerly for *Yield to the Night* to be released, little did she realise that her headline hogging would lead to her being voted 'Variety Club, Show Business Personality of the Year' in early 1956.

Meanwhile, everything was auguring well for *Yield to the Night*. The film was chosen for the 1956 Royal Command Film Performance, enabling Her Majesty to find out first-hand just how sinister the part was. On top of this, it was the only British film chosen for the Cannes Film Festival.

Although *Yield to the Night* was not a Rank production, John Davis decreed that the Rank players should attend. This time, Diana did not attend a film festival as part of a bevy of starlets, but as one of the country's leading stars.

With the other Rank stars, she was installed at the

grandiose Carlton Hotel. Once again it was the round of film shows and official 'sight-seeing', accompanied by the statutory hordes of press photographers.

Knowing that the cameramen were clamouring for pictures of her in a bathing suit, she worked out another little strategy. The more they asked her to go to the beach, the more she refused – until, that is, the day she knew a rival contingent of Continental stars was due to arrive at the festival. Then she went! The result was that while she posed for the gentlemen for as long as they wanted, the other stars arrived unnoticed.

Diana had no cause to worry about rival actresses at the première of *Yield to the Night*. At the flood-lit cinema, cameramen jostled with guests reluctant to take their seats until they had seen 'the star' of the evening. When Miss Dors eyed the reception committee, she paused and then muttered under her breath:

"Wet your lips, breathe deep – and – here we go, boys."

Then she swept into the heart of the mass with never a blink as the flash bulbs went off like sheet lightning.

"This was indeed my night. The crowds thronged outside the cinema as I drove up in my powder-blue Cadillac which matched my evening gown. Inside, the atmosphere was electric. Director J. Lee Thompson was sitting beside me, and tears were unashamedly running down his face, for he had lived and breathed the film for so long, and we all knew it was good. At the end, the audience rose as one and applauded and then cheered."

Diana had claimed for herself the recognition she had always craved as an actress, in the light of which Hamilton's scheme for her as a sex goddess paled, in her heart of hearts, into insignificance.

Yield to the Night was released on June 12 1956. By then Diana had already booked her passage to Hollywood and the fulfilment of all her childhood dreams. The Bob Hope spectacular turned out to be the stepping stone she needed. After seeing it, Bob Dozier, head of RKO Pictures, came up with the suggestion that the British actress team up with George Gobel, who, though unknown in Britain, was America's biggest comedy star, in the hope of making a movie viable on both sides of the Atlantic.

Diana, though, delayed her departure until the British première of *Yield to the Night* at the Haymarket. After its acclaim in Cannes, where it was short-listed for best picture, none of its connections had any doubts that the film would be well received, and that the dumb blonde bombshell on whose central performance the film relied, would no longer be considered dumb.

One critic summed up the reaction of the rest:

'Let me say at once that Miss Dors, with her cherubic features shining with anguish and lack of make-up, her fabulous curves shrouded in a shapeless prison nighty, puts up a splendid show, proof that her mink bikinis need no longer be the only wear.

'So good is she that after the initial wonder of finding her in so serious a picture, I cease to see Diana Dors at all, but only Mary Hilton. Indeed it was a remarkably restrained performance from a star whose public and private life was so blatantly the opposite.'

After the opening, the Hamiltons invited many from the audience to accompany them back to Bel-Air, the name they gave to their home in Maidenhead. Among the guests were Rex Harrison, Anna Neagle, Roger Moore and producers and directors such as Otto Preminger and John Huston. Personal friends Patrick Holt, Sandra Dorne, John Pertwee and Jean Marsh were also in attendance. But it was Kim Novak who commented:

"Bel-Air is better than anything I have ever seen in Hollywood."

It was more like a palace than a Victorian mansion. Around the 83 ft long swimming pool, lion and tiger skins were liberally sprinkled on the scarlet and duck-egg blue carpet, and over it Hamilton had built a penthouse full of tapestries, huge mirrors and chandeliers. On the thick pile carpets stood chairs which looked more like thrones. The squash courts had been replaced by a cinema, and a rock pool had been built, with giant framed photographs of Diana all around. Bel-Air was a worthy setting for a champagne reception.

Diana had much to celebrate: recognition as an actress, a new exquisite luxury home, and her forthcoming trip to Hollywood. As she lifted her glass, her thoughts must have gone to Sir Carol. Working for him had been the turning point in her acting career.

In life you make your own luck. Behind the actress's success was both her and her husband's determination that she should succeed. To be Britain's answer to Marilyn Monroe meant being number one. Diana did all she could to keep ahead of the rest of the pack. Whether it was in Venice, or Cannes, or posing at the wheel of her Delahaye two-seater sports car, Diana dared to be different.

She and Hamilton had a matchless flair for publicity. It was a well known fact in the business that the Hamiltons never employed a press agent. Diana and her husband planned and organised things to hit the headlines. Far from relying on revealing photographs of three vital statistics, $36\frac{1}{2}$–24–35, and a height in stockinged feet of 5 ft $5\frac{1}{4}$ inches, which made her a leading pin-up girl, they both brilliantly exploited the slightest opportunity for publicity, subscribing to the theory that the only bad publicity was no publicity at all. Hamilton's adage had been from the beginning, "It doesn't matter what they say as long as they spell the name right."

Diana, too, had the knack of making quotable quotes and, once in the limelight, was able to hold her own with anyone.

At the same time the star learnt never to believe in her own publicity. She was quite aware of her failings. She knew her much-photographed figure was good – but no more remarkable than many others. She was a master at striking a pose that would accentuate her good points and camouflage her not-so-good ones, or at finding those eye-catching circumstances that made any deficiencies in her figure seem insignificant. Every item of clothing she wore drew attention to her bosom and wiggle-walk.

"To succeed in showbusiness," she claimed, "you need some basic ingredients — a lot of luck, a lot of guts, a skin like a rhinoceros, the patience of a saint — a little talent helps."

Talent, then, was the final ingredient in the success recipe. And this was too often lost sight of amid the glare of flashbulbs. It needed someone with a discerning eye to notice it. Kenneth Tynan, Ken Annakin, and Sydney Box certainly did, and Carol Reed had been in a position to bring it to the fore.

Now it was Hollywood or bust!

7
"A WANTON HUSSY"

Yield to the Night had brought Diana Dors a satisfaction no other film had. It had fulfilled a craving inside and allowed her ability and talent as an actress to shine out. Her hope now was that the great British public would accept her as such.

But it was not to be. To them she could not be other than their very own blonde bombshell. That is what her own publicity had turned her into. She was Britain's answer to the very best anyone else could offer, and they were proud of her, too. She had the looks, that 'come on' glint in her eye, the hourglass figure and the 'wiggle'. 'La Dors' was a sex-symbol.

Diana was sensible enough to realise, though, that she would never have had the chance to demonstrate her talent as an actress had it not been for Hamilton. It was he who made her a familiar face with the public, 'nice little actress' though she was. Without him she would have been lost, amid the myriad starlets to whom Rank had handed out contracts.

So though part of her hated all the publicity, Diana realised that getting into the news was necessary. As Hamilton had told her so many times, there was no money in just being an actress, but there was plenty in being a sex-symbol. Where else but in Hollywood would she be offered £30,000 for a movie, plus £200 a week's expenses for herself and her husband?

On June 18, after a lavish champagne party in Diana's honour in the state suite of the *Queen Elizabeth II*, the ship set sail from Southampton. Five days later, the Manhattan skyline beckoned and the Statue of Liberty became a timely reminder that for anyone who had a will to succeed, America offered the freedom and opportunity to do so.

RKO's publicity machines had worked well. Within hours

of her arrival, the people of New York knew that Britain's own sex-symbol was in their midst. The headlines of one paper said, "Britain's Dynamite Explodes on the City", and another, "A Fascinating Fabrication of Femininity". A third wrote, "Miss Dors is here competing for the world's glamour spotlight on Marilyn's home ground."

But the British girl had no liking for this comparison with Marilyn, despite the fact that RKO made it very much a part of their publicity blurb. At the Sheree Netherlands Hotel Diana pointed out that she had been making films since she was fourteen years old and was known in England long before Marilyn Monroe made her début in 1950 in *The Asphalt Jungle*. She also said she had read somewhere 'how very much like our own Diana Dors is Marilyn Monroe'.

Diana wise-cracked with her guests for more than three hours. Sipping a mint julep, she flitted from table to table giving three interviews a minute. When two television reporters crossed microphones, she made everyone laugh by pushing them gently aside and saying, "Careful boys, you're covering what I'm selling!"

Diana's stay in New York comprised interviews and more interviews, picture sessions for glossy magazines, and being photographed wherever she went. After a few days the Hamiltons flew out to a similar reception at the swanky Beverly Hills Hotel in Los Angeles. It was so crowded that Diana could be forgiven for thinking the whole of Hollywood had turned up. Among the more influential were Hedda Hopper and Louella Parsons, who had the reputation of either making or breaking the career of any aspiring artist. Hamilton immediately tried to ingratiate himself.

"Miss Hopper," said Hamilton, "I cannot see, now that I've met you, how you could possibly deserve the reputation of being unkind to anyone."

"OK Hamilton," Hopper replied, "Don't overdo it."

This was a rare rebuff for the Hamilton charm. Diana, on the other hand, passed her gruelling test with honours, which very much pleased the heads of RKO.

To welcome her, the studio had filled the room with flowers and presented gifts: a cine-camera and a British bicycle. When William Dozier, the head of the studio, heard she had no mink, he promptly had a selection of mink stoles delivered to the studio. Diana picked out a breathtaking silver blue one. Dozier put it around her shoulders. "There you are. That's a present from me and my wife. You look stunning."

Before shooting began on *I Married a Woman*, the English star met the people on the set and underwent a series of make-up and dress tests.

When filming started, she was most impressed by the all-round professionalism of the studio. The care and trouble everyone went to astounded her. There was no question of stopping for tea breaks as in England, and lunch was taken if and when it was possible.

As for star treatment, Diana had never experienced its equal. A uniformed chauffeur came to pick her up in the morning and drive her through the wide, sunlit, palm-tree'd avenues to the studio. Very different from driving through the dark, cold and often foggy streets of London!

Diana was quick to overcome her fears of the press, and of working with people she did not know. She also struck up a very happy and easy working relationship with George Gobel and director Hal Kanter, and reminisced a lot about England with co-star Jessie Royce-Landis, who had appeared on the London stage. Hal Kanter, who had directed many a famous face over the years, was greatly impressed by Diana's professionalism, and somewhat taken aback at an intelligence not often found in sex goddesses.

The hand of friendship was extended to the Hamiltons by everyone they met in tinsel city. With seven films in production at the same time, it was natural that a relationship would be set up with fellow actors and actresses. Debbie Reynolds and Eddie Fisher were making *A Bundle of Joy*, while Donald O'Connor and

Buster Keaton were collaborating on *The Buster Keaton Story*. Other stars on the lot included Katherine Hepburn, Ginger Rogers, Donna Reed, Kirk Douglas, and the young James McCarthur, son of Helen Hayes.

An important contact too for Dennis and Diana was the English contingent, who seemed to use the mansion of James and Pamela Mason as their base when in Hollywood. Among these were actor Scott Forbes, and Stewart Grainger and his wife, Jean Simmons, who lived on a ranch in New Mexico.

Parties, big and prestigious, where everyone who was anyone got invited, were on-going events. One of the first people Diana met at these, and with whom she developed a lifelong friendship, was Liberace.

Not far from RKO were the Paramount Studios and Diana was able to renew her contact with old friend Bob Hope. Bob's agent, Lou Schurr, had done a lot of behind-the-scenes work to persuade RKO to engage the English girl. Almost straight away he put plans into operation to try and reunite the partnership that had fared so well on television. What he had in mind were a couple of films based on the old Jean Harlow vehicles, *Blonde Bombshell* and *Platinum Blonde*.

Naturally these vibrations soon reached RKO. They had already been impressed by the way Miss Dors was taking everything in her stride. Diana began to lay down conditions. She insisted on a closed set, and got it. Then she said that she would only appear on the Ed Sullivan television show if she got paid. Because this was a peak viewing time programme, other artists willingly appeared for nothing. But not so Diana.

Thinking that they might have a hot property on their hands, Bill Dozier drew up a contract to make their relationship permanent. The deal was for three pictures. The first would pay Diana more than £30,000, the second £40,000 plus, and the third about £50,000. And that on top of £35,000 for the present movie.

Hamilton was jubilant. The first thing he decided to do was buy a permanent residence, now that they would be spending more time in Hollywood.

Diana was against the idea. For one thing, she loved her rented accommodation, which afforded a splendid view of the surrounding countryside. It was a compact, modern home, and being that little distance away from Los Angeles, more private than most. She did not consider it prudent, either, to splash out money when so much of their cash was invested in property at home. Dennis would not be disuaded, however – a sign of the growing conflict between them.

Nevertheless the Hamiltons found the first few weeks in Hollywood quite exhilarating. It lived up to all the razzmatazz they had read about. They loved the open spaces, the wide avenues and distance between houses, so different from the compactness of 'little ol' England'. The beauty of the mountains, the orange trees, the palm trees, the azure blue of the sea and the continuous sunshine made it a veritable paradise. Even so, during the long warm evenings sitting on the patio beside the softly lit swimming pool, the scent of jasmine and gardenias filling the air, they found themselves talking about home.

The drive-in restaurants, ice cream parlours, hamburger-stands and hot-dog joints were as nothing compared with the village pubs they used to frequent – The Bell and Dragon at Cookham and The Plough at Waltham St Lawrence.

Diana missed the luxuriant green of a cooler climate, the rain, and even a simple walk; every American owned a car and drove everywhere, and pedestrians were regarded as poor, odd, or, in most cases eyed with suspicion as up to no good.

She missed their friends, too, and back home she was treated as a normal person and not just a carbon copy of Marilyn Monroe.

The conversation was more blatantly cinema. Stars in Holywood talked almost continually about themselves, their contracts, their homes and the last picture they were in. At one party, Diana overheard a star talking to a reporter about herself for over half-an-hour. Then quite suddenly, she said brightly,

"That's enough about me – let's talk about you. What did *you* think of my latest picture?" Diana began to tire of the relentless triviality.

It did not take long for Dennis to see the danger-signals. He always pre-empted any discussion about going home by talking of how much money could be made in America. The RKO contract was proof enough of that. He also put renewed effort into buying a Hollywood home. During his house hunting, he bought her a brand new 'Lincoln' convertible, reputedly the best car then on the road in America. This time Diana was able to drive it, having at last passed her driving test in the spring.

By early August, Hamilton had found the home he wanted: Hillside House, which was situated in the exclusive Cold Water Canyon area. As usual, it was the best money could buy, and reputed to have cost over £35,700. On the strength of Diana's contract with RKO, the studio loaned him money to buy it. Once purchased, the house was used to repay hospitality. The Hamiltons wanted to show off the house, naturally, and also to introduce their friend, Mr 'Teasy-Weasy' Raymond, London's foremost hairdresser, to the Hollywood set and so launch his career in America with a party. He persuaded Diana to say that she was going to pay him £3,000 to fly over and create a new hairstyle especially for her. The press loved it.

Workmen laboured all weekend under the broiling sun to prepare for the party. They fixed bars under the Jacaranda trees and dotted the swimming pool with blue carnations. Mr Teasy-Weasy, as always, wore a blue carnation in his lapel.

On August 19, 250 guests came. It was a glittering affair. Raymond's name floated in giant flowers on top of the swimming pool. A band played at one end while champagne flowed non-stop at the other. Columnists and photographers mingled with stars happily posing for pictures. Among those present were Zsa Zsa Gabor, Ginger Rogers, Dinah Shore, Liberace, Lana Turner, Greer Garson, Doris Day, Eddie Fisher, Debbie Reynolds and many other screen names.

Diana, dressed casually in a check blouse and tight Toreador pants, was happily chatting to her guests. Unbeknown to her, a photographer with a ready eye for a scoop decided in advance to engineer one. With the party concentrated around the swimming pool he had no difficulty in pushing Diana into the water. He made the mistake of lingering too long taking his pictures, enabling Hamilton to exact vengeance in the only way he knew. The beating up of the unfortunate man made headlines the next day: "GO HOME DIANA AND TAKE MR DORS WITH YOU". The couple were labelled unsavoury Britons, "who should know better than to come to our country and behave like hooligans". The press almost to a man defended their own. Up until this incident the Hamiltons had been able to do no wrong. now all of a sudden the honeymoon period was over.

RKO celebrated the completion of *I Married a Woman* with a lavish party. As far as they were concerned, they were well satisfied with the way the film had worked out.

William Dozier travelled with Diana and Dennis to San Francisco to film *The Unholy Wife*. The film was set in the heart of the Californian wine-growing region. The director was John Farrow. He was married to film star Maureen O'Sullivan. Of their seven children, Mia, their daughter, continued the showbusiness tradition by becoming an actress.

Farrow was a strong personality who enjoyed the reputation for striking terror into the hearts of those who worked with him. Sensing Diana was no sycophant, he immediately struck up a good rapport with her. He even employed a guitarist to serenade his leading lady between takes.

Again, filming progressed favourably. But because of the continued jibes in the press, Dozier began to have deep misgivings about the viability of his blonde star. The harassed studio boss was in for another shock. His leading lady fancied her co-star.

Almost as soon as she began working with Rod Steiger, Diana became infatuated with him. Rod Steiger was everything Hamilton was not: sophisticated, clever, intelligent, and never at a loss for words. But above all else he treated her as a woman, something Dennis Hamilton had never done. Steiger's acting, and his dedication to his art, too, only made her admire him the more.

As the weeks went by the relationship deepened, and the British star could not conceal her feelings any more. She told Dennis, and the next day in a fit of envy he chased Steiger around the set with a shot-gun. This explosion of anger only served to substantiate rumours of the romance, and in the 1950s it was anathema for any star to be found dallying in the extra-marital bed. The press made the most of their chance for good copy.

The studio did all they could to get both parties to play down the affair. Hamilton came up with what he thought was an astute move, telling his wife that he was flying back to England. He hoped that the panic of having to live alone in a large mansion would bring Diana to her senses. To his amazement she went with him to the airport, not, as he thought, to travel home, but simply to help him onto the plane.

Hamilton's departure was, in fact, a great relief to Diana. His behaviour was becoming increasingly disturbed. More and more he had ranted and raved and stormed around the house like a bull, smashing any furniture in sight.

His absence allowed his wife's liaison with Steiger to proceed unhindered. Both Steiger and Diana threw all caution to the wind, and whatever advice and admonitions came their way fell on deaf ears. Now, stories which had been circulating in the papers and denied by both Dennis and Diana were backed up with the tangible evidence of photographs.

On his arrival in England Dennis laughed off the rumours of the affair and, when challenged with photographs of his wife and Steiger at their mountain retreat embracing one another, said:

"They're publicity stills. It's all nonsense. Diana's on contract to Rank. She'll be flying back to London on November 3 to begin filming *The Long Haul* with Victor Mature."

Nevertheless, Dennis promptly returned to Hollywood to do his best to cover up the scandal. With him went the editor of the

News of the World to conclude a deal for Diana's life story.

Once Dozier knew of Hamilton's arrival, he insisted, on pain of dismissal, that they should pretend to be together. "You'll just have to give the performance of your life," he told the besotted star.

Condemnation of the affair was coming from all sides, most vociferously from the Women's Catholic Guild of America. They spoke of the English actress as a "wanton hussy who should get back to England before she causes any more contamination".

Both stars now had to endure the agony of enforced separation. Steiger was sent away to a hideaway in Malibu, while Diana stayed in Beverly Hills. When they were eventually allowed back on the set, there was no question of a tête-à-tête between shots. They were made to wait in separate caravans.

Hamilton, seeing he was getting nowhere with his wife, returned to England. Left alone in a great mausoleum of a house, Diana wondered where all those friends she had made were. What had happened to all the invitations she once had a struggle to fit in to her schedule? Hollywood, that same Hollywood she had dreamed about since she was three years old, was not what she expected. Too many stars lived in fear of the people who pulled the strings. Diana Dors was a disaster area, and not many people wanted to be seen in her company.

As filming of *The Unholy Wife* came to an end, and Rod Steiger moved back to New York and his wife, Diana knew their relationship was over for good. To add to her misery RKO were being very slow to take up their option on the next film.

News had also leaked that *I Married a Woman* was poor and in these circles you are only as good as your last picture. Diana had no alternative but to return home to England and honour her contract with Rank.

At London airport, she was given a tremendous homecoming by reporters. Instead of Berkshire she made for London and the Dorchester Hotel. Journalists followed her there and, although tired from travelling and the culmination of weeks of trauma, Diana held a press conference.

She looked well, with her suntan and lighter hair emphasised by the dark suit she wore. Losing extra pounds because of Steiger had made a shapelier figure too. Nevertheless, Diana was subdued. Half hidden behind large diamante studded sunglasses, she played with a lucky charm on her necklace. Reporters noticed that she was not wearing a wedding ring.

"Diana without Dennis is going to be different," she said in an earnest voice. "My mink bikini era is over. All that stuff, the practical jokes, the swimming pools, the fun and games, were really more Dennis than me.

"The house in Maidenhead with the swimming pool – that belongs to Dennis. I can manage to live without a swimming pool. Dennis is welcome to it.

"I've been growing up. My outlook has widened and broadened. I've done a lot of thinking lately. I hope I won't be hitting the headlines as much as I used to. People must be as fed up with reading about the exploits of Diana Dors as I am."

When asked it there was any chance of a reconciliation, the star was evasive:

"I don't know that one can just pick up where one left off – I wouldn't like to say."

Hamilton knew he had to talk to his wife. He knew too that without money her stay at the Dorchester would be short. It was not long before a silver-blue Cadillac glided up to the hotel to take her back to Maidenhead for a 'quiet talk'. That talk lasted 36 hours, after which an elated Hamilton informed the weary men of the media that there had been a reconciliation.

8
FUN AND GAMES
AT MAIDENHEAD

On the first day of a new film, Dennis always sent his wife a good-luck telegram and a large bouquet of flowers. Although Diana had always appreciated the gesture in the past, when filming *The Long Haul* began it no longer meant much to her. They were back together, but as far as she was concerned, it was because she had no choice. One advantage of the Rod Steiger business, however, was that Diana had loosened the stranglehold Hamilton had over her. She yearned now for the freedom to control her own destiny, and indeed for a man she could really love and respect. She felt neither for her husband.

There were far too many essential differences between them for a lifetime together. Moreover, there were still too many scars from the Steiger affair for the gap between them ever to heal properly.

Diana took the chance of a couple of days off to visit her father in Swindon. Mr Fluck, too, in his own way had become a bit of a celebrity. Reporters regularly asked him what it was like to be the father of Britain's most highly paid film star.

This short time at home with her father afforded Diana a haven of peace in the midst of public and domestic storms. Auntie Kit, who was housekeeping for Bert, doted on her niece and insisted on tucking her up in bed beneath the green counterpane, just as she had done when Diana was a tot.

The school in the Bath Road was still in the hands of the Misses Cockey. They had certainly not changed their feelings about the local prodigy. When one reporter went to the little school there were no photographs of Miss Dors on the walls.

"You see," they explained, "we do not need that type of publicity here. We think Diana is an extremely clever girl, oh, extremely brilliant even. But we also think she has spoiled herself. You know the sort of thing... portraits in papers that are, well, so difficult for us to describe... er, so revealing!

"We want the children to be proud of their school. We try to give them a nice background. We are not eager that they should boast 'ours is the school Diana Dors went to!'.

"We have never seen her on the films, but I know that our elocution teacher, Miss Leason, who taught Diana here, went backstage at a play in Brighton and told Diana that films had spoiled her style.

"Such a pity. We are very particular here about elocution. Diana had splendid training!"

Auntie Kit was interviewed too:

"The men like her, but the women are jealous. But Diana never really liked this place. She was always determined to get away. You know, she was so terribly devoted to her mother; they did everything together – that's why she rarely comes home now.

"What is there for her here now? I am here – but it's not the same, and it hurts her so much to come. She really loves her dad – do you know, she even taught him to make a champagne cocktail! But it's her mum she misses."

Diana enjoyed working with the muscular Mature on *The Long Haul*. Because he had quite a reputation with the ladies, Hamilton came to the studio, but in his zeal to hold on to his 'meal-ticket', he guessed wrongly. The insecure and unhappy actress turned rather to Tommy Yeardye.

Tommy was Victor Mature's stuntman on the film. Living in fear of her husband's tempers, Diana was quick to respond to this six-foot three-inch dark-haired Irishman, who treated her with respect and admiration. As each working day passed she enjoyed being in his company more and more.

Feeling he had come to an understanding with Mature, Hamilton concentrated on property deals. The latest acquisition was a property by the riverside at Windsor which he had turned into a club, calling it 'El Dors'.

On April 1, there was a surprise in store for Diana. Before taking his wife to the studio for some night filming, Dennis suggested they go to a show. He drove her to the King's Theatre, Hammersmith. Cameras suddenly swung in the audience's direction and to the seat in which the blonde was sitting. She was the unwitting subject of 'This is Your Life'.

It was a nostalgic trip. Bert Fluck, Auntie Kit and three uncles appeared. Also present was her elocution teacher, Miss Leason. Eamon Andrews introduced Donald Zec, the *Daily Mirror* columnist, saying that he knew there were many flattering things which Zec could say about Diana. "But... The spot we've put you on is quite different – it's to do the opposite. It's all yours."'

Diana laughed: "I'd better leave, I think."

Donald took a deep breath.

"Dear me," he said, "oh well, let's face it, Diana, you represent the most calculated, hard-boiled exploitation of sex I've ever seen in British pictures."

Zec paused. "Do you want me to go on?" he asked.

"Not really," laughed Diana.

"Everything you say, everything you wear, everything you do is calculated to create a very big sensation... Sensations like falling into swimming pools – by accident."

"Let's not go into that," said Diana.

It did not deter Zec.

"And wearing mink bikinis – which I don't think was an accident!"

"Yes," butted in Diana, "I also remember your remarks on it."

"Although I think at times you are brash – perhaps at times very outrageous – I would also like to think you are unique.

"No one can ignore Diana Dors. You have that rare quality which I admire and which I write about all the time... you are a star."

Diana rose, clasped his hand. Zec kissed her.

There was one big surprise for Diana, and that was kept to

the end of the programme. Stewart Sawyer, the Hollywood photographer involved in the pool incident, came through the curtains.

"Diana, I've travelled 6,000 miles to shake your hand."

Compere Eamonn added, "All the way from Hollywood to reassert his innocence."

Diana immediately quipped, "If I'd known you were going to be here, I'd have worn my bathing suit!"

Dennis became tense at the appearance of the photographer. He clenched the arms of his chair. When the curtain rang down on 'This is Your Life', Diana, with red book in hand, found herself hard pressed to prevent her husband doling out another beating.

The actress endured a miserable week at Maidenhead. At the end of it, to her utter amazement Hamilton told her quite calmly that he was leaving her; that he had fallen in love with someone else. Diana could not make up her mind whether Hamilton meant it, but he did go, and the days passed.

Feeling lonely and fretful in the ominous stillness of the place, Diana phoned Yeardye. The stuntman came to Maidenhead and they went out for a drive. On their return to the penthouse, the housekeeper came rushing out to Diana.

"Mr Hamilton is here and insists on talking to you."

"You'd better go," said Yeardye, "after all, he is your husband."

Hamilton, knowing full well he had lost his hold on his wife, was money-conscious enough to make contingency plans. When Diana entered the mansion and the door was closed, he burst upon her brandishing a shot-gun. Pointing it menacingly, he forced her into the nearest room and then turned the key in the lock of the door. As Diana stood quivering with fright, he pushed the barrel of the shot-gun through the window with a smash of glass.

"You", he shouted at Yeardye, "Get going. This is my home and this is my business." Then he produced a piece of paper and flung it at his wife.

"Here, Dors. Sign it."

The paper listed everything Diana was to sign over to him: virtually all the property, apart from the penthouse and the Cadillac, which he had given her as a present, plus every penny she had in the bank. The actress did as she was told, and moved nervously towards the door. But Dennis, venting all his anger, punched her in the head.

Yeardye, who was keeping his eye on the window, heard shouts and screams. Approaching, he saw Dennis beating Diana up. Rushing into the house, he found the door locked. Pushing his fist through a glass panel, he opened it from the inside and, mindless of the shot-gun, flung himself at Hamilton. The dazed Diana looked on as the two men grappled on the floor. For the first time in his life Dennis was on the wrong end of a beating as the brawny Irishman laid him to the floor. With tears running down his face Hamilton looked up at his wife.

"Dors, how could you do this to me? I love you so much."

This scene brought down the final curtain on their marriage. The penthouse, which had been the scene of so much unpleasantness, was too much for Diana to face. Tommy took her to his parents' home in London, but it soon became apparent that with Diana's wardrobe she could not continue to stay at the Yeardyes' very long. She rented a small mews house in Belgravia.

When *The Long Haul* ended, Dennis sent his wife £1,000 from the £20,000 he received for her services. It was obvious that legal proceedings would have to be taken to safeguard her interests. The first step was to draw up a petition for divorce, and Shirley Ann Field, the girl he said he was in love with, was cited as co-respondent. Eventually, it was agreed that, despite the fact that Diana's 'shot-gun statement' had been signed under duress, the only property she was entitled to was the penthouse, the Cadillac and her personal belongings. Furious as she was at being swindled out of a fortune, she was helpless to do anything about it. As regards the penthouse, it was stipulated that she should live there without further harrassment from her husband. Taking no chances on that score, Tommy Yeardye returned with her to act as bodyguard.

Much as she wanted to move out of the penthouse, there was no way she could. Hamilton had commandeered her salary. The star made sure that for her next film, which Hamilton had negotiated, she would get the full fee. It was set in Italy, and so it meant spending at least three months in Rome. Tommy and Diana flew over in early July, while the Cadillac, driven by a friend, was taken across to Italy so they could use it during their stay.

La Regazza Del Paliso, in which Vittorio Gassman played opposite Diana, was about the famous horse race, the Palio, which had been run in Sienna for over a thousand years – a violent affair, with riders lashing at each other with bull whips.

It was in Rome that the British girl regretted her impulsiveness in linking up with Tommy. She knew that he had been the innocent victim of circumstance, and that it was not his fault that he had been caught up in her domestic affairs, but as Bill Dozier very plainly remarked: "It is very important to have something to talk about when you finally fall out of bed." Tommy was like an oak tree – tall, solid and strong, but silent.

Back in Maidenhead again for the autumn, the rivalry between Diana and Dennis knew no bounds. First Dennis would throw a party. The next night Diana would throw an even bigger one. As the guests arrived, factions from over the way would yell insults from the windows.

When all was quiet both protagonists would spy on each other, Diana invariably from a keyhole in the door of the fence that separated them. There was always plenty for her to see. Dennis had turned part of 'Woodhurst' into a gambling casino where his guests played chemin-de-fer and roulette.

Cars roared down from London at any hour of the day, bringing starlets who hoped that Dennis would make them into sex bombshells as he had Diana. Once when one lady friend unexpectedly turned up while he was entertaining another, he hid the first outside the French windows. Diana saw the girl wandering forlornly in the grounds, and began speculating how often that must have happened when she had come home from the studios earlier than expected.

Diana returned from a short trip to America, where she had appeared on the 'Perry Como Show', to learn that she had been handpicked by director Gordon Parry to play the steamy Calico in his latest film *Tread Softly Stranger*. This was welcome news, as was the salary of £20,000 she would receive. The star was in financial straights, owing thousands of pounds in back taxes to the Inland Revenue, which Hamilton had conveniently neglected to pay. Approaching J. Arthur Rank, she found the Corporation was prepared to give her £7,000 if she terminated their contract. In desperation Diana accepted their offer; in her heart she knew that they had no plans for her.

On Boxing Day 1957, Diana threw one of her most extravagant parties. Everyone who was anyone was invited. Producers, directors, writers, comedians; her friends included Patrick Holt and Sandra Dorne, and Michael Caborn-Waterfield, who felt more free to visit now that Dennis had left. A young up-and-coming comedian, Dickie Dawson, whom Tommy and Diana had met doing his turn at London's Stork Club, was particularly on form. The dark, wavy haired, rather dapper young man with a brilliant smile regaled the guests with jokes and impersonations of famous stars – including Rod Steiger!

The party went with a swing. But by the time most guests had left, there was a great commotion next door, down by the river's edge, where the whole sky seemed to be lit up: Dennis's yacht *The Breeze* was going up in flames.

Hamilton was away that evening. When he returned and found it completely gutted, he was inconsolable. Immediately he suspected someone from Diana's party, and blamed Tommy Yeardye.

Hamilton took up the cudgels with his wife. He ransacked

the penthouse when its occupants were out, tapped telephone calls, and hurled bricks through the windows. Diana and Tommy had no alternative but to endure all this until the completion of *Tread Softly Stranger*.

Most of the fee from *The Girl Who Rode in the Palio*, the film she made in Italy, had paid off back taxes, but with the money she received from terminating her contract with Rank plus her fee from *Tread Softly Stranger*, Diana was able to buy a farm at Billingshurst in Sussex. After six torrid years with Hamilton, the relative peace and quiet of leafy Sussex suited her. While she spent her days supervising the alterations and additions to her country mansion, Tommy passed the time sunbathing. For exercise he lifted dumbbells, or rode the horse she had bought him.

Diana heard about a film called *Passport to Shame*. Anxious for a part in it, she agreed to a fee far below her going rate: £8,000 for a support role. The lead went to French actress Odile Versois, who played a French girl being white-slaved by Brenda de Banzie and Herbert Lom, with Eddie Constantine and Diana trying to rescue her.

Diana had come to a crossroads in her life. The Hollywood disappointment has been a real blow. Had her two pictures there made money, she would most certainly have been accepted as an international star. Instead, they marked her decline. *I Married a Woman* was so bad that it had not yet been released, and *The Unholy Wife* came out as a second feature. Further, RKO had not come up with the other two films they promised.

Then *The Long Haul* got a terrible mauling when it was released, as did *Tread Softly Stranger*.

The muck-slinging that went on between the rival factions at Maidenhead, and the burning of the yacht, made far from desirable headlines and had the effect of keeping producers and directors at arm's length. And though she denied it, she was finding it difficult to make a mark without Hamilton at her side. Gone were the flair and exuberance that had turned a little provincial actress into the daring, glorious, irrepressible Dors.

One thing she had learnt from Hamilton, though, was that when times were rough there was always cabaret. Up and down the country there were still variety theatres and cinemas specialising in one-night stands.

Knowing Diana had little to do, Joe Collins, her variety agent, got in contact. He very much wanted to take 'The Diana Dors Show' on the road again, and Diana's commitment to *Passport to Shame* was such that she would be free by July. Tommy was not keen on the idea, but there was very little alternative. Besides, Diana was beginning to find country life boring. When the star, Yeardye and her agent got down to planning the show, they decided they needed a top notch comedian-cum-compere to play off against Diana. The blonde wanted Digby Wolfe, but surprisingly the normally taciturn Yeardye insisted on Dickie Dawson.

'The Diana Dors Show' took to the road in early August 1958 to great acclaim. A good deal of credit for this was due to Dickie Dawson's brilliant script. Dickie knew the tour with Diana Dors was a real scoop for him, and he worked hard to make the most of it. He was buoyant the whole time, amusing Diana with his jokes and mimicry, both on and off the stage.

He made up his mind to marry her. Diana, was quite content to just sit back and let it all happen. She had always been a sucker for humour and charm, and she enjoyed Dickie's perpetual patter which contrasted attractively with Yeardye's quietness. And when he told her he loved her, she said she loved him too.

With reporters buzzing around during their tour, Dickie Dawson made their feelings public knowledge.

It was left to Diana to break the news to Tommy before the newspapers did so. He had been in the audience during opening week, but soon got fed up with watching the show night after night, and returned to the farm. Diana telephoned and broke the news to him. He was very angry:

"You're a fool to fall in love with Dawson. He'll turn out just like all the other men in your life."

It was when the Variety Show reached the Finsbury Park Empire that Diana was told that her husband was ill and had been taken to the London Clinic. On her way to visit him, she herself became violently ill too. A replacement was found to fill her top of the bill spot. Diana was later told she had pancreatitis and was warned that if she wished to live, she should go on a special diet.

She finally got to see her estranged husband on October 13. Such a celebrity had he become in his own right that there was always a crowd of newsmen at the London Clinic to report the comings and goings. When she got to his bedside, he was in a highly emotional state, repeating over and over again that the doctors had only given him a few years to live.

"That can't be!" said Diana, "What's wrong with you?"

"I have a heart infection. The bastards are giving me twenty injections a day."

"Thousands of people have heart complaints," commented his wife. "My father was given ten years to live in 1941, and he's still going strong. You'll just have to slow down when you come out; take life at a quieter pace."

"You don't understand, nobody understands." Hamilton buried his face in the pillow and sobbed uncontrollably.

When he had calmed down, Diana learnt that he had moved to a small mews flat in Belgravia. Since her departure, he had been deprived of a regular source of income, save that which came from the 'El Dors' Club. Diana could not help feeling sorry that it had all been downhill for him since the spring. His worries and setbacks, as well as his ill health had furrowed their impressions on his face.

Diana's twenty-seventh birthday arrived. Invitations to a cocktail party went out – not to celebrate her birthday though, but for the launching of a new shampoo. No doubt memories of that Drene shampoo advert all those years ago, had prompted this!

Hamilton was allowed out on the condition he take things easy. Within hours of release, he went to 'El Dors' and beat up the manager, whom he believed was swindling him of money.

Meanwhile, Diana's lawyer began drawing up another divorce petition. The earlier one citing Shirley Ann Field had been withdrawn in the summer, because of Miss Field's denials. Even though Dennis had his bad days when he cried a lot, believing the whole world to be against him, he had not quite lost his old sparkle. When Diana's lawyer asked him for a list of his infidelities, he wrote back saying he would write them down only if the lawyer had a spare week in which to read them.

In December 1958, Diana and Dickie flew off to South Africa to do a short cabaret season in Johannesburg and Durban. Diana was only too happy to flee the winter's cold, take in the sun, and earn £1,000.

Back at home, there was an offer to appear on the Steve Allen Television Show in New York. This particularly delighted Dickie. It had always been his greatest ambition to go to America.

In the New Year of 1959, while Diana was busy packing to leave, she received a phone call. Hamilton was back in the London Clinic.

"I'm off to America in the morning," Diana told him, "but I'll see you when I get back – in about a month."

"No, Dors, I'll not be seeing you again."

'Why ever not? Come on Dennis, pull yourself together. You upset us all when you talk like this."

"I will not be here when you come back," he said quietly but firmly. Then, dropping his voice to a whisper: "Goodbye, darling. Remember, I love you."

When Diana reached America, she soon involved herself in rehearsals for the Steve Allen Television Show, which at the time was the biggest of its kind. The audience loved her. Whereas she had failed on the Western seaboard, she succeeded on the Eastern seaboard, and was contracted to appear in three more shows throughout the next few months.

While in America she decided to use the opportunity to go back to Hollywood and renew old acquaintances. She stayed a while with Liberace at his lush and extravagant Palm Springs home.

It was there that she received news of her husband's death. Diana returned home at once, accompanied by Dickie. She read in the papers about the man who had remained an enigma to her:

'What did he really accomplish – this man who died alone at the weekend?'

Another read: 'Dennis Hamilton, 34-year-old-high-living playboy, died owing money to many.'

Despite owning a Rolls Royce, nine companies, a coffee bar, other properties, and a £10,000 yacht, precious little would be left by the time his many creditors had staked their claims.

When Diana learned of the funeral arrangements, she was more than a little suprised. By all accounts, Dennis had become a Roman Catholic just nine days before he died, and the requiem was to be at the Catholic Church of St James, Spanish Place.

The Funeral was more like a star-studded premiére, with hundreds of people both within and without the church. Women in particular came in droves. There were many of the couple's mutual friends from their early years – Michael Caborn-Waterfield, Patrick Holt and wife Sandra Dorne, John Pertwee, to name but a few.

But it was a sombre and sad widow who knelt alone during the 40-minute Mass on February 3. Just one floral tribute topped the purple canopied coffin: hers – a four-foot-long cross made up of red roses and lilly-of-the-valley. The inscription on the memorial card read:

"To my darling Dennis, with loving memories that words can never express."

What Diana did not know until the next day was that her husband had died of tertiary syphilis. She was not after all surprised; he had always been a womaniser. Knowing the cause of his death helped her to understand his irrational and unpredictable behaviour. His neuroses, delusions of grandeur and his persecution complex all made sense in the light of this disease, which had been eating away at him even before he had met her.

She could not help reflecting fondly on their life together, though, the years of happiness and unhappiness, their escapades, adventures and almost continuous reckless and riotous living. It is true he exploited her, and swindled her of a fortune – but he had also, as he said he would, made her a star.

9

THE WINDS OF CHANGE

"This is as bad as making a film."

Twenty-eight-year-old Diana Dors laughed as she kissed Dickie Dawson for television, film and still cameramen.

As the actress cut the three-tier white and pink wedding cake she was heard to say above the general hubbub and popping of champagne corks, "I'm so happy. It was all over so quickly and I still can't believe I'm married."

It was April 12, 1959, and the Harwyn Club, New York's most exclusive night spot, was jam-packed with well-wishers. In contrast to this, their wedding just an hour or so before had been a very quiet affair. The ceremony took place in a friend's riverside apartment directly after the Steve Allen Show, in which Diana had star billing. A New York State judge presided. It took seven minutes and was attended by just eight people. Diana wore a close fitting gold lamé dress covered with cream silk.

Indeed, events had taken place at whirlwind speed. At Christmas Dickie had presented her with a diamond ring, insisting on setting the date. She felt that she did not want to rush into marriage. For one thing, it was too soon after Hamilton's death. But she was completely overruled and Dickie went ahead and made all the arrangements. In just eight weeks Diana had been estranged, widowed and married again. Dickie, unknown to the public less than a year ago, was now the husband of a national property.

On April 17, their homecoming was reported in the papers.

"We are going to concentrate on farming and very soon a family," said Diana. "If we are lucky enough to have a baby I would give up everything."

Dickie went on to explain what 'everything' was: a

four-month tour of America by Diana with her own revue and a
39-instalment American TV series. When asked what was in the
immediate pipeline, Diana said:

"Dickie and myself will start preparing for 'The Diana
Dors Show' to go out on ATV in three weeks' time."

Dickie began to script the show. Two Americans, the
husband and wife singing team Jack Cassidy and Shirley Jones,
were booked for a guest appearance. The show proved a great
success. Diana impersonated Marlene Dietrich, Eartha Kitt,
Clara Bow and Marilyn Monroe, as well as singing, dancing and
performing sketches with Dickie.

They were booked for another. This time their guests were
friends Patrick Holt and Sandra Dorne and the brother and sister
partnership, Lionel and Joyce Blair. Some of the sequences for the
programmes were shot at Billingshurst. Viewers had the chance to
see the beautiful 14th century mansion, and Diana down at the
farm with some of the animals.

While filming the second show Diana discovered she was
pregnant. Her new husband was delighted at the prospect. So too
was Diana who, at the age of twenty-eight, was anxious for
parenthood.

Thinking ahead to when his wife would be unable to work,
Dickie hired a new agent to arrange a quick succession of cabaret
engagements. As a result of the success of Diana's TV shows he
also suggested a record album. Wally Stott's Big Band was chosen
to accompany her and the star cut an LP which included the
classics, 'The Gentleman Is A Dope' and the Nat King Cole hit,
'Let There Be Love'.

Soon Diana was off abroad again. She appeared at Cannes,
and played to packed audiences at the Palm Beach Casino, then in
Italy, and Spain.

Back again in England, they put the farm on the market
and in its place they bought a modern, spacious single-storied
building at Virginia Water, Surrey. The first addition to the house
was a golden-walled nursery ready to receive Dors junior; this time

the swimming pool was to take second place. With the frilly white crib now standing in readiness and a room set aside for a nanny, husband and wife discussed names. It was decided that should their first born be a boy they would call him Mark Richard – Dickie's choice – if a girl, Caroline Jane.

Expecting to be sidelined now, Diana, very much to her horror, found herself making front page news. The editor of the English newspaper who had come to Hollywood with Dennis Hamilton to buy the rights to Diana Dors's life story now felt the time was right to publish it. Her first thought was that at twenty-eight years of age it was a mite premature. Nevertheless, without even looking at it, she gave her consent to the script that Hamilton had commissioned some three years earlier. She had been offered £35,000.

What Diana did not realise, though, was that her 'life story' was a cheap and salacious account of the worst extremes of her time with her first husband. Much was made of how the latter had the 'guest' rooms at Maidenhead bugged and took delight in playing back their occupants' conversation over breakfast. His *pièce de résistance* was a two-way mirror that he installed under the floorboards above the main guest room. This was circular, about 4 ft in diameter, and sunk into the middle of the floor. Among the half-dozen or so guests Dennis invited at a time, there was always some stage-struck girl, overcome by both drink and the company of film people, who would lose her virtue in the guest room, while Hamilton quietly led the rest upstairs to watch what was going on below.

When the 'exclusive' was published in January 1960 it caused a furore that lasted for months. The abuse that ensued was far worse than anything she had endured in Hollywood. With a condemnation too from the Archbishop of Canterbury, who denounced her as a wayward hussy, Diana's reputation as a scarlet woman was well and truly sealed.

The people of Swindon, formerly so proud of their protégé, took umbrage too. The correspondence columns of the local press were full of the controversy. The star, whose halo had not only slipped but had fallen right off, was quick to retort to the barbed comments of the people of her home town:

"Swindon can go and jump in its own railway yard."

It was hard for Bert Fluck. What he felt most keenly, as a religious man, was the condemnation of his daughter by the Archbishop of Canterbury.

But amid all the scandal Dickie and Diana had the birth of their first child to look forward to. For the time being, Fleet Street concentrated on the fact that Britain's one and only sex-symbol was about to become a mum. Even the most meagre tit-bits of news concerning their plans for the baby were splashed across the tabloids.

The big day finally arrived on February 4 1960, at 9.55 in the London Clinic. At the end of twenty-seven hours' labour, the overjoyed mother held her baby in her arms.

The next day Dawson held a press conference: Mark Richard had tipped the scales at a healthy 6lb 15oz, "And that's just his head," he added, laughing.

"Why, he's this big," he stretched his arms apart. "He has black hair, like mine, and the loveliest eyes. Diana's wonderful."

Dickie then excused himself and went off to pick up a more intimate expression of his love. His selection was a lovely gold bangle-bracelet, with a medallion on which he had inscribed, "Darling, thank you for Mark. Love, Dickie."

The Dawsons took their first-born home to Virginia Water.

Within a month of their son's arrival, Dickie flew off to America. On the strength of his wife's success on the Steve Allen Show, there had been talk of her appearing in Las Vegas. His mission was to negotiate a contract for this. On the British side of the Atlantic, things were far too hot for the sex-symbol-cum-mother. Baroness Stokes made the front pages when she suggested Diana Dors was unfit to be a mother and that the baby should be adopted.

With a contract worth $7,000 a week, Dickie returned to

England to fetch his wife, and he left her in no doubt whatsoever that from now on, she would be a working mum. The thought of leaving her beautiful baby behind, made Diana feel sick at heart. The actress's only consolation was that Mark Richard would be in the hands of a loving and capable nurse.

Diana considered herself lucky to have found such a treasure as Amy Baker. The minute this tall lady, her hair in a bun, set eyes on the infant, she obviously loved and cared for him. The slightest whimper from the child sent her scampering to the dainty frilled lace crib. Many a night, Diana through sleepy eyes saw Miss Baker, dark hair unleashed from its pins hanging to her waist, cuddling the baby.

"I'll guard him with my life," Miss Baker assured the tearful mother as Diana said goodbye to go to America. Then lowering her voice to almost a whisper, she said, more to herself than the child's mother, "I knew from the moment he grabbed hold of my little finger that he was mine...."

The Dawsons stopped over in New York to enlist the services of a musical director, and flew off to Los Angeles to rehearse at the home of Liberace.

The show opened with Diana doing three spots a night: the Dinner Show at 8 pm, the next at midnight and the last at 2 am. At the end of two months, having had not a single night off, Diana was worn out. She missed a couple of shows because of illness, but at heart the real trouble was that she was pining for her baby.

Dickie, though, had been enjoying life to the full. Las Vegas was a new experience for him. He gambled, met leading American comedians, stars and gangsters. He was slow to sense his wife's growing restlessness. When the club wished to renew her contract for another month at an extra $10,000 a week, Diana considered turning it down. Dickie acted at once. One evening, when the platinum blonde returned to her suite after the dinner show, Dickie was waiting to greet her:

"Di, there's a lawyer waiting to see you. He's going to try and get some money out of RKO for the contract of yours they cancelled!"

Dickie led her into the adjoining apartment. There stood Amy Baker holding in her arms the gurgling four-month-old, blue-eyed, golden haired Mark Richard. Diana cried as she cuddled the beautiful child in her arms. When Dickie said that the nurse and baby were there to stay, it was the only argument she needed to get on and do another month of nightly stands.

After the Las Vegas engagement, Diana was anxious to get back to England. She was very much looking forward to seeing her new indoor swimming pool, which had been built at Virginia Water, and the cinema, too, now ready for use. Dickie, though, had other plans. The comedian had accepted an offer of $12,000 a week to appear twice nightly at Lake Tahoe on his wife's behalf, and after that, had fixed a fortnight's stint at Ciro's along Sunset Strip in Hollywood.

Back in Hollywood, Dawson, as good as his word, went straight off to RKO to get the half million dollars they still owed on Diana's 1956 contract. With a team of lawyers battling on behalf of the plaintiff, the studios could procrastinate no longer. She received $70,000 compensation.

An offer then came her way to appear with a host of other British stars in the Danny Kaye vehicle, 'At the Double'. This followed an overture from Jerry Lewis to appear in his next film, *Ladies Man*. Free from Hamilton's clutches, she seemed once more to endear herself to the American public. It all came as something of a surprise to the British girl, who, after her dismal assault on celluloid city some four years earlier, never intended going back to Hollywood, let alone appearing in a film being made there.

Work was coming her way at a much greater rate of remuneration than she could have hoped for in England, and Dickie decided to set up home in Hollywood. Diana was against it, but he was adamant. So the Dawsons, and nanny Baker, moved from the rented mansion of the legendary Greta Garbo, to one of their own at Benedict Canyon, Beverly Hills.

Diana's connection with England was finally severed when

their home at Virginia Water was sold. A delighted Dickie flew back to England to tie up the loose ends and to sell off the contents. Once the decision had been made to stay in the States, there had been really very little choice. The Beverly Hills home cost $175,000. The money from RKO helped, but it still left the Dawsons with a big mortgage.

One advantage of living in Hollywood was that they had many friends there, including Bob Hope and Liberace, and Diana spent many a Sunday at the home of Pamela Mason. Terry Thomas, with whom she had worked in her early Hamilton days on the television series 'How do you View', came to stay with them. He was in Hollywood working on *It's a Mad, Mad, Mad, Mad World* with Stanley Kramer, and was a continuous source of amusement for the English girl.

Dickie, on the other hand, became very morose. Rubbing shoulders with famous showbiz people made him more conscious of his own lack of success, and of the fact that he would not be mixing in these circles had it not been for his wife. Newsmen referred to him as Mr Dors. Hoping to have taken America by storm as a comedian, he had been disillusioned. Hollywood was full of talented comedians and the competition too intense for Richard Dawson, as he now wished to be known.

In the early spring, they returned to England with baby Mark and nanny Baker. Diana's agent had negotiated a part with Lionel Jeffries and Kathleen Harrison in *Mrs Gibbon's Boys*. While in London, Diana's hospitality to Terry Thomas was returned when he allowed her to use his apartment in Belgravia. At the weekends they stayed in Swindon, where Amy and Mark were staying with Bert Fluck and Auntie Kit.

It was quite an ordeal for Mr Fluck, who was not in the best of health. He found Amy intolerable.

"God save me from that impossible woman," he complained, as Diana left Marlborough Road, "she's clearly a very good nanny, but," he warned his daughter, "she's no great friend of yours."

Back in Hollywood, Dickie could find no work, much as he tried. Diana, on the other hand, was soon off to wherever work happened to be. It might be a guest appearance on a TV show in New York, where she was always popular, or a guest star appearance in a TV series like, 'The Racers'; it could be a nightclub in Texas or Nevada, or even further afield, as for example her South American tour.

Yet when she returned exhausted to Beverly Hills, there was rarely a warm welcome. It seemed that as far as Amy was concerned, Diana was a rival for Mark's affections. The boy would invariably tug at the skirts of his nanny when mother approached. If Diana tried to go off with her son for a picnic, the woman threw a tantrum.

In September 1961, Diana went off to Spain where she was scheduled to do a film for $75,000. Because of lack of finance filming came to a halt after just two weeks. By way of compensation, Diana was offered another film, *King Of The Roaring Twenties*, to be shot in London. This time, the ailing Bert Fluck refused to have Amy to stay. Diana had no alternative but to find accommodation for herself, nanny and son, and so she rented a mews house not far from where she had stayed with Terry Thomas, whose visits provided light-hearted relief from the unpredictable nanny.

Afterwards Diana returned to their American home, and at Christmas, Dickie flew over to join her, and in the early part of the new year 1962 he helped his wife during her cabaret appearances.

She had some good news for him. She was pregnant again, and the baby was due at the end of June. Gary was born on June 27 1962, in the Cedars of Lebanon Hospital, Los Angeles. He weighed in at an enormous 10lb 2oz. Once again their new arrival drew the camera lenses when he was wheeled to the waiting limousine on his mother's lap. Pamela Mason, Liberace, Steve Allen and Terry Thomas were godparents at the christening.

Within ten weeks of Gary's birth, his mother was on the road again. For a natural mother, the continuous work and travel was a tremendous burden, but someone had to pay the mortgage. Dickie, oppressed more than ever by a sense of failure, was withdrawing into himself, cutting himself off from her.

In the winter of 1963, Diana was in England again for a cameo role in *West Eleven* with Hamilton's old mentor, Eric Portman. During this trip, she came across Michael Caborn-Waterfield who was now doing very well for himself. Diana proudly showed off the photographs of her two sons.

In Swindon, Bert Fluck was pleased to see the photographs and his daughter, but he was very frail. Diana was not to regret her visits for it was while appearing in cabaret in New York in April 1963 that news reached her of his death. He was 69 years old.

When Diana telephoned Auntie Kit, she learnt that her father had passed peacefully away in his sleep at about 2 o'clock in the morning. Her aunt also insisted that her niece should not cancel her undertakings in New York to return home for the funeral. As money was low and commitments were high, Diana agreed, but she deeply regretted it later.

Her next contract was the lead in a musical, *The Pyjama Game*, a Broadway and West End hit in its time, but now booked for a summer season in New Jersey. There was also a guest appearance in a television show programmed in Ohio.

Afterwards, Diana insisted on a really good holiday. The Dawson entourage made for Hawaii, but despite the beautiful surroundings, Dickie was as withdrawn as ever, and Amy continued to rule the roost.

After the holiday, Diana was booked on an Australian tour. On her arrival at Perth the grand welcoming party included a brass band, soldiers on parade and even a police escort.

The following days were spent rehearsing and publicising the Diana Dors Show. It was hard work again, but the star of the show did not seem to notice. She was regaining something of her old vitality and *joie de vivre*.

Only one thing could have caused this transformation, and that was love. As often happens when someone is treated with indifference, the door is left wide open for another to come in and provide the love and attention which is missing. That person was Darryl Stewart, the dark curly-headed support artist on the bill.

Life with Darryl was idyllic. Perth was not the dusty sheep-rearing place that Diana had imagined all Australia to be. It was as green and rambling as England, with roses, pubs and elegant houses. The only difference was that the sun shone all day; October was the beginning of the Australian summer.

Much as Diana was rejuvenated by Darryl's company, there was one fly in the ointment of their relationship. He had two young children and a wife in Sydney, who was expecting a third. Diana decided, however, that while in Perth she would live for the moment.

She was blissfully happy, but time flew by. Christmas 1963 was almost upon them; it was time to go home. Not being able to stand the thought of being apart, she made arrangements for Darryl to come to Los Angeles.

Diana felt guilty about carrying on an affair behind Dickie's back. She hated all the secret meetings, messages, phone calls. It was hard, too, on Darryl, who had nothing to do all day but wait in his apartment for his mistress to contact him.

Then Dickie intercepted a letter and found out. The blow up resulted in Diana hastily petitioning for divorce on the grounds of mental cruelty.

At heart she knew she would never marry Darryl. It would have spelt heartbreak for all concerned: for the wife alone at home waiting for the husband to call, for the man pulled both ways....

Almost immediately she had cold feet about her divorce petition. How would Dickie live? She knew he was still finding work hard to come by. She thought of the children. The petition was withdrawn. With the birth of the Stewarts' baby imminent, Darryl decided to go back to Australia, but before leaving, arrangements were made for the lovers to meet later in England, where Diana would be filming *Allez France*.

Back in London, she took out a six-month lease on a small

cottage in Chelsea to prepare for Darryl's arrival. But like Gil, the Norwegian blonde, Darryl did not turn up. He wrote to say he had to postpone his visit. When Diana got over the shock of it, she put pen to paper herself in a scathing reply.

'I'm not prepared to go on living a love affair with a telephone and a writing pad. Either you come here now, or not at all.'

Sure the ultimatum would bring her recalcitrant lover to the front door, Diana waited. She was not to hear from Darryl again!

Diana had more spunk than just to remain at home and wallow in self-pity. She threw a party. Shirley Bassey was there, among many stars, and Michael Caborn-Waterfield too. Diana found herself enjoying the company of Troy Dante. Dante was a product of the 'Swinging Sixties'. He was young, in his early twenties, and desperate to jump on the pop star bandwagon. The cheeky Cockney was given the key of Diana's house in Chelsea, while she went to Paris for some location shots of *Allez France*.

Troy was married, but Diana was out on a limb now with no husband, no love in her life, and in desperate need of some affection, and she let this need override everything else. Troy Dante remained with her on another tour of nightclubs; this time it was Italy, an ideal setting for a budding romance.

A bombshell awaited Diana on her return. Her agent had dropped her. Moving up in the world, he now had on his books stars of the calibre of Elizabeth Taylor and Richard Burton, and he saw no showbiz future for Diana Dors.

Diana found it increasingly hard to cut her cloth to size. She still loved expensive clothes, luxurious surroundings, lavish entertaining, and to go everywhere in a large American limousine. Creditors began sueing. To pay her debts, and keep up the kind of life she was used to, Diana took any work that came her way. She appeared in 'Gay' clubs – where her glamour gowns were particularly appreciated – in working men's clubs, or in anything else that came along. The plush, softly lit surroundings of up-market night spots were replaced by the red brick of surburbia. Diana had to perform under fluorescent lights with rows of formica-topped tables stretching out around her. Beer-swilling men shouted:

"Get 'em off. Show us your tits!"

Meanwhile, Dickie had abandoned all hope of making it as a comedian, and had gone back to acting. He landed a part in *King Rat* with George Segal. Then followed a television serial called 'Hogan's Heroes' in which he was cast as a conniving Englishman in a POW camp during the Second World War. The series proved very popular, and for its new runs Dickie's salary got bigger and bigger.

Now the roles of husband and wife were reversed. But Dickie's generosity did not extend to paying for Diana to fly to America. No longer able to pay for herself, let alone Troy, Diana was forced to remain in England.

1967 proved a traumatic year. The Inland Revenue presented her with a bill for £48,413 for unpaid taxes going back to the year 1957. With just a small part in *Berserk* with Joan Crawford, and one or two brief appearances in TV plays to supplement her one-night stands, there was no way she could pay the enormous bill.

It is typical of Diana that, in spite of bankruptcy staring her in the face, she sought out her solicitor with a view to buying a very lovely property that had gone onto the market at Sunningdale, Berkshire, not far from her old Virginia Water haunts. She mentioned insurance policies that long ago she had put into a trust fund in England for her boys. With that cash they would have a home to live in if they ever decided to come to England. The solicitor though, would have nothing to do with this suggestion, and neither would Dickie.

Diana added a tax consultant to her list of advisers. His first suggestion, on learning of the size of the celebrity's tax bill, was to urge her to sell her Beverly Hills home to pay it off. Any money left over should be shared equally. And that would certainly mean she would also have enough to purchase her own home.

Worried lest he should lose his 'castle', Dickie very soon came up with an alternative solution. As they had been separated for so long, the easy answer, he said, was a divorce – so long as she did not contest his petition and agreed to give him the house, all its contents, and legal custody of the children. That way the Inland Revenue would have no claim on the property, as it would not be in his wife's name. In return Dickie would allow her access to the insurance policies.

Diana was reluctant to agree to giving him legal custody of her beautiful boys, but after a great deal of thought she came to the conclusion that in order to safeguard her family in America she really had no choice. She made two provisions: that she have access to her children at any time, and that Dickie put the mansion in trust for the boys to ensure the home was theirs should he ever marry again.

She knew in her heart that it would be better for them to stay in a country they knew and loved, with a father who doted on them, and a nanny who, despite her funny ways and possessiveness, was truly devoted to them. The only other option was for them to come to England, live in hotel rooms, and see their mother prostituting herself to cat-calls and jeers on stage for a cheap laugh.

With Dickie's assurances that all would be well, she agreed. At the same time it was sanctioned that the money which she had placed in the trust fund for Mark and Gary could be used to purchase a house. To expedite matters, Dickie made a rare visit to England where, in a lawyer's office, Diana signed over to him everything she had worked so hard for. She could not help but remember another such signing session with Dennis Hamilton.

In order to shake off her depression, Diana chased up the directors of the trust and had them buy the house she had decided on. Orchard Manor was a magnificent mock Tudor mansion standing in three acres of ground.

As luck would have it, a substantial part came her way in the film *Hammerhead* with Vince Edwards. This enabled her to furnish her home before all her assets could be swallowed up by the official receiver. This she did *à la* Hollywood with gilt chairs, gilt-framed mirrors, pictures, and turquoise and gold upholstered furniture.

The centrepiece was a huge stone farmhouse-style fireplace similar to one she had very much liked in her Billingshurst days. This curved round a corner of the drawing room to form an attractive cocktail bar, complete with running water and sink.

It was too hard to relinquish the old style. "A film star has to live up to her image," was an adage of Hamilton's. This Diana made her own.

Orchard Manor in Sunningdale, positioned as it was at the end of a long leafy lane, was private and peaceful. It made an ideal place in which to settle after her recent traumas. Its calm atmosphere helped her ponder the future and, no doubt, rue the times she had been so stupid with her money.

The England Diana Dors had come back to was very different to the one she had left when she went to Hollywood some twelve years earlier. It was no longer the age of the sex-symbol. What she had got up to on the Grand Canal in her mink bikini would now only make people laugh. Full frontal nudity was commonplace in the cinema.

The days of glamour were over. The flat-busted Twiggy was the model of the moment. With the arrival of women's lib and unisex, the girls in pretty dresses gave way to the uniformity of jeans.

One bright spot in the otherwise worrying and depressing summer of 1968 was the arrival of Mark and Gary, accompanied by nurse Amy Baker, to spend a holiday with their mother in the new home.

It was then that the thought struck her that perhaps they could live part of the time in England. She could see no reason why this would not work. As the idea grew more positive in her mind, she had a chat with Amy, who in turn said she would pass it on to the children's father.

The minute she set eyes on Dickie Dawson, however, Amy had quite a different tale to tell. Mrs Dawson, she said, had tried to stop them returning home, to keep them in England permanently – and against their will.... So colourful a picture did she paint that Dickie Dawson decided that his children would never visit their mother in England again.

After thirty-seven years, life had virtually ground to a stop for Diana Dors. It was time to sit down and take stock. She knew that it was not the bankruptcy, the bad publicity or the scandals she had to endure which upset her most, but the fact that she had made such a mess of her emotional life and was a failure at marriage.

"I'm a victim of my own image," she told a reporter who came to Orchard Manor, "and it makes it almost impossible to think about ever having a normal, happy love affair. It is just one of those hard cold facts you have to face sooner or later. And it makes the future look pretty bleak!"

Diana Dors as a comparative screen novice (no blonde hair yet!) as she appeared in *Diamond City* with David Farrar, Honor Blackman and Niall McGinnis. The year was 1949 and Diana was a supporting player only. Roger Bray produced and David MacDonald directed this South African "Western".

A young Diana Dors with an equally young Anthony Newley in a scene from the 1949 comedy-drama *A Boy, A Girl and a Bike*.

Diana Dors visits the prop department at Pinewood Studios and measures up to the Grecian plaster casts made for a historical picture of the time. This picture was taken in 1954.

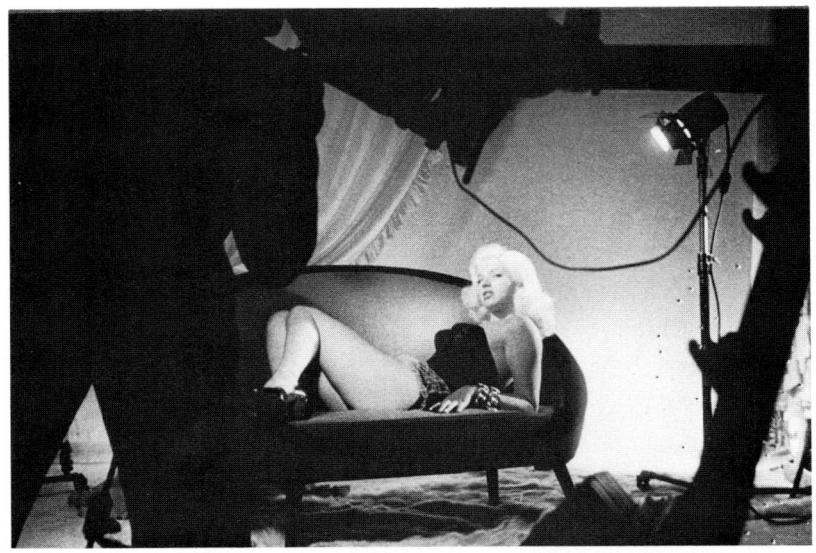

**Posing for glamour shots is hard work. Diana Dors strutting her
stuff for a pin-up in the defunct London magazine, 'Illustrated'.**

**Diana Dors (checking her own measurements?)
caught off-guard during a magazine picture
session in London in 1956. The icebear
was also enjoying it.**

**Diana Dors getting ready for a fashion magazine layout in
1956, London.**

Posing for endless publicity shots in the fifties sometimes became tiring — especially when photographers ran out of ideas and thought of a lawnmower.

Diana Dors and Rod Steiger in a scene from the murder mystery, *The Unholy Wife*. It was claimed at the time that a rumoured romance between her and Steiger broke up her marriage to Dennis Hamilton.

Diana Dors attending a Sammy Davis Jnr. opening in Hollywood in 1960 with husband of the time, Dickie Dawson. Diana was in Hollywood to co-star with Jerry Lewis in *Ladies Man*, but the role failed to materialise when she opted for *On the Double* with Danny Kaye instead.

10

THEN THERE WERE THREE

"How do feel about guesting in one of the episodes in a new TV series I'm doing?"

"What's the series?" Diana asked producer Jim Goddard

"It's called 'The Inquisitors' . . . it's it's about a psychiatric-detective. The part I'm offering you is that of a nightclub stripper."

"Hmm. Well, darling, at the working men's clubs I do, they practically strip me off anyway . . . their eyes come out like organ stops," she laughed. "So it'll hardly be anything new, will it? Anyway, who are the stars?"

"Two very good actors," he replied, "Tony Selby and Alan Lake."

At the latter's name, her heart fluttered and she accepted the offer to be guest star. She had seen Alan Lake recently in *Thief*, a television play. He resembled Troy a little; lithe figure, dark curly hair, with a roguish look about him, and she had been impressed by his acting. Now as she thought about it, it struck her that she was more than just a little attracted to this man she had yet to meet. From that moment on, Diana never stopped thinking about him, so much so that the night before rehearsals were due to begin, she even dreamt she had fallen in love with him.

The next morning, October 10 1968, she rose early, paid more attention to her dress and make-up than she did her breakfast, and then set off to work. On her quick journey to the M4, she passed the lush, cosy homesteads of the stockbroker belt where Georgian houses with odeon brickwork and continental eaves remained partly hidden behind banks of laurel and pyramid-shaped cypresses.

Today's work, though, would take her to the far from

congenial surroundings of an old Territorial Army hall near Bond St Tube Station in London. There she was to do her first readings for 'The Peeling of Sweet P. Lawrence'.

Alan Lake was not at all impressed when told the guest actress's name.

"Oh, no! Not Madame Tits and Lips!"

The reputation of film stars was a poor one in the industry at this time. They invariably arrived late, forgot their lines and generally caused chaos. He determined to out-act the woman he considered to be just a brainless sex-symbol. But the young, brash Alan Lake was in for a surprise.

As it happened, it was he who arrived late. His taxi had been caught up in traffic. The guest star was sitting quietly on a wooden chair in a corner of the hall, wearing spectacles and studying her lines. She had on a simple wool two-piece, and a red leather coat, with her blonde hair gently caressing her shoulders. She looked sensational.

She laughed when Goddard related the young man's original comments about his co-star for the episode, and Alan's stomach did a somersault.

Diana's reaction was the same. For, although she had always admitted to being easily attracted to people, this was different to anything she had experienced.

Alan and Diana found they wanted to be alone together, to talk together. During a break in rehearsals they went off on their own and had a pub lunch.

The following day they continued to work naturally and easily together. And when once more they went to the nearby pub, three of Diana's friends were waiting for them. Alan knew instinctively that it was no accident. The glamorous blonde was obviously parading him for approval.

That evening they went to Trader Vic's for dinner. Diana was no drinker, but she kept up with Alan as he downed his favourite cocktail, 'Scorpions', a drink made from several kinds of rum served with crushed ice and topped with a gardenia.

"From the menu," Alan remembered later, "we chose 'Vic's titbits'—we laughed about the name with various references to chest measurements—which consisted of chestnuts, bacon rolls, barbecued pork and spare ribs."

Drink she was unused to gave Diana the courage to ask the question which was plaguing her:

"Are you married, Alan?"

He shook his head.

"But there must be some woman about to throw herself off a bridge because of you?" she persisted.

"There is no one," he answered quietly.

After the meal, they moved on to a nightclub.

"By the end of the evening," Alan recalled, "the staff were piling up the furniture around us. We hardly noticed. We only had eyes for each other."

Alan Lake's assumption about film stars in general, and Diana in particular, had evaporated. The actress's first script readings had been of high quality, and now he knew she was as witty a raconteur as he, and an altogether excellent conversationalist.

The following day, during night filming at Wembley Studios, Alan Lake proposed. They were sitting in a car holding hands for a scene, and between takes he said:

"I want to tell you I love you and I want to marry you."

Then he took a ring from his pocket.

"My uncle bequeathed this to me before he died. It's a Mexican antique. He said I had to promise to give it to the girl I was going to marry."

Alan gently ran his fingers over the amethyst set in silver and then raised his large brown eyes and stared unblinkingly at the actress.

"And this is what I'm doing. I love you and I want to marry you. I've never said that to anyone before."

"But we've only known each other a few days," she protested feebly.

133

"Yes, I know that. But what I feel is that I've known you all my life." And, taking her hand, he slipped the ring onto her finger.

Things could not happen quickly enough for Alan. He had never been married and she was legally divorced, so there was no reason to delay. But what about Troy? He had to be told. The next day, Alan went down to Orchard Manor to sort the matter out. Troy had already gone.

When Alan told his mates he was going to marry Diana Dors, they were stunned. The odds were stacked against such a marriage. In their eyes, Alan was not the type to settle down. He was a person who enjoyed his freedom. Alan refused to listen and decided that, before announcing their engagement to the press, he would take his betrothed home to his native Stoke-on-Trent to meet his family.

Cyril and Millicent Lake were amazed when their son 'phoned to say he was bringing a girl home. Alan had had plenty of girls but he never took one home.

While they were wondering how Diana Dors would react to their modest home, Alan's older sister, Vilma, had something else on her mind:

"My first thoughts were her age. You see, I still thought of Alan as my baby brother."

But the star completely bowled them over with her naturalness and warmth – none more so than Vilma and her husband Ken. Away from the glossy public image, and dressed very simply, Diana came across as an honest, straightforward down-to-earth person.

That evening the family enjoyed a sing-song at the local before the couple returned to Sunningdale and the press, where Diana and Alan publicly announced their engagement. The showbiz world was taken by surprise. Everyone believed Diana to be still married to Dickie Dawson. At the press conference, Alan said:

"It was love at first sight. She is a very rare person. She made me respond. She is very warm, which is something you don't find nowadays."

When the inevitable subject of money came up, Alan laughed about his bride-to-be's £49,000 bankruptcy debt. He pointing to the earring in his left ear and said:

"I think she is only marrying me for the gold in this!"

Diana laughed too:

"Well, I may be earning more than Alan at the moment, but I believe the position will soon be reversed."

"What about the difference in your age, then?"

"Well," said Alan, "when one falls in love it doesn't matter about ages. It is completely irrelevant."

Diana wrote to Dickie Dawson, telling him of her engagement and the date of the wedding, hoping he would send her boys over for the ceremony. She received no reply.

On November 23 1968, just seven weeks after their first meeting, and the day before Alan's twenty-eighth birthday, they were married at Caxton Hall. This time, unlike the two previous very rushed affairs, Diana looked like a bride. She wore a white mini-dress covered by a most beautiful all-lace cape with scalloped edges, and she carried a bouquet of orchids. The bridegroom was the height of fashion in a black velvet suit and a white frilled shirt. They were surrounded by their families and friends and a battery of cameras and newsmen who followed their every move. The reception took place at London's Astor Club and went on throughout the weekend.

While their friends drank and toasted their health and happiness, there were others who took a cynical view of their marriage. Some accused the twice-married Diana of trying to prove to the world that by marrying a man nearly ten years younger then herself she still retained her sex-symbol appeal. Others accused Alan of being an ambitious opportunist trying to make a name for himself on the back of a legend. There were very few in the show business world who expected their marriage to last more than a few weeks. Dickie Dawson took the same casual view of the wedding and did not inform his sons. They were shocked when they saw their mother's wedding relayed on newsreel.

While Alan continued filming *The Inquisitors*, Diana worked hard at establishing a home at Orchard Manor. The happy couple were not long in residence when she discovered that she was pregnant. Alan was delighted, and resolved to work even harder to support her. Not yet in the star bracket, he was determined nevertheless to keep her in the style to which she was accustomed. In the meantime, Diana made the most of the rare opportunity to relax and prepare for her baby.

Alan Lake had wanted to be an actor from as far back as he could remember. He was born on November 24 1940, at Milton, a village not far from Stoke-on-Trent. At the early age of five, Alan made his stage début – at the bottom of the stairs in the family home. Vilma, his sister, recalls it very clearly:

"At that time they used to have 'Carrol Levis' Discoveries' on the radio, and Alan used to appear from behind a curtain he'd rigged up, and we all had to give him a big hand, because everyone had to give Carrol Levis' discoveries a big hand. He did his little turn. He used to sing: then, of course, you see, in his mind he had been discovered, and it was from that moment he decided he was going to be an actor."

Alan had to wait until he became a teenager before he could take the next step to realising his dream. He joined the local drama group, the Milton Players.

"Mum and me had to go to every production. He always seemed as if he was overacting because he was so good. I mean, we realise now that he was so good." recalls Vilma.

"Academically, he was average. He couldn't be doing with school. He was in music festivals from school. He had the most beautiful soprano voice, and then, of course, his voice broke, but he still kept appearing in the drama group.

"He left school and had several jobs. First he went to work in an office, which he hated. Then he decided he'd perhaps like to be a joiner, so he had all the tools. But no, that was no good for him either, and all the time he was getting on with drama, which was

becoming more and more important. And then he went to the
Royal Academy of Dramatic Art on a scholarship, the only boy in
his year to do so."

The first thing they concentrated on at RADA was to rid
the aspiring actor of his Black Country accent, something he was
always to resent, particularly in his 'angry young man' days.
Alan's innate talent, ability and determination kept him among
the front-runners at RADA, and he won the Academy's award at
the end of the year for the most promising pupil.

When he had finished his course the principals of RADA
asked him to stay on as a tutor. This he did, and taught stage craft
and fencing for two years, until his appetite for the 'real thing' led
him into repertory.

'Hereward the Wake' marked his television début. 'Dixon
of Dock Green' and another television series called 'The
Pretenders' followed, and he made his first film appearance in *Sky
West and Crooked*, where his Romany looks secured him the part of a
gipsy boy.

Since then his career had followed the upward climb to the
lead role in 'The Inquisitors', and as Diana looked forward to the
birth of her child, he went back to his first love – the theatre.

Alan's ultimate ambition was to produce and direct.
Ideally he wanted his own theatre and company, "to get rid of the
middlemen, the spies and the sycophants". It would also offer a
way of "getting back at the system" which he envisaged as a
highly self-protective clique.

Alan interrupted his rehearsals at the Fortune Theatre,
where Alun Owen's play *There'll be Some Changes Made* was soon to
open, to be at the bedside of his wife when Jason David was born
on September 11 1969. He could hardly believe that in less than a
year, he was not only a married man but a proud father, and he
revelled in it all.

Jason was christened at Sunningdale Church. Vilma
Thursfield, Alan's sister, was his godmother. This time, Mark, Gary
and, of course, their nanny, Miss Baker, came over from the States.

After the christening, the boys posed for photographs beside mum, with Alan holding the baby.

The two young Dawsons were able to stay over Christmas until the New Year of 1970, when school restarted and they had to return to the States. It was with heavy heart that Diana saw them off at the airport. Alan, who had taken to the youngsters as they had to him, was also upset. He had become accustomed to having them around the place, and when not at rehearsals he spent hours playing games with them and taking them riding in nearby Windsor Great Park.

With Alan in a starring role at a London theatre, Diana was overflowing with happiness. The proud wife and mother wanted nothing better then to stay at home and be just that.

Donald Howarth's *Three Months Gone* was in the offing at the Royal Court Theatre, and it was from there that the author phoned Alan Lake to interest him in the leading part. Alan read the script, liked it and accepted the role. It was also suggested to him that his wife play the part of Mrs Hacker, a blowsy, loudmouthed, sexually gluttonous widow approaching the menopause.

Seventeen years had passed since Diana Dors had appeared on the West End stage. Since then, all she had to show for her acting ability was *Yield to the Night*, and from there on, the best décolletage in the business had been exploited for all it was worth. The challenge of *Three Months Gone* was too tempting for a woman who wanted to be treated as the serious actress which, in Hamilton's day, she had not been allowed to be.

Diana signed on, saying to Alan:

"I'm sure it will help our acting together, being married, and knowing each other's moods and reactions so well."

Three Months Gone opened at the Royal Court Theatre in January 1970, and was an overnight success. Diana Dors, a showbiz joke, was quite suddenly the toast of the town.

The reviews for both Alan and Diana were glowing. In particular the critics were more than generous to Diana. The theatre critic of the *Sunday Observer* was particularly apposite:

> All these plaudits for Miss Dors show an image can dog
> you all your life. She's been lumbered as a sex-pot since she
> made her first film, when she was fifteen. She tried to shake out
> from time to time. Her portrayal of a condemned woman in
> *Yield to the Night* in 1956 thrilled the critics but not the
> producers. As she says, she was the nearest thing to sex the
> British cinema had then and it didn't want to part with a good
> thing. Kenneth Tynan directed her first stage play back in
> 1953. And it looks like the career of Miss Dors has changed in
> this direction once more.

That, of course, was Diana's aim. The man in her life was a
top class actor, his recitation of his parts at home reminding her
what it was to live in an actor's milieu. Alan was as erudite in his
art as Steiger had been, and this stimulated Diana further. The
bookshelves in their living room were filled with the complete
works of Shakespeare and all the classics of drama and poetry. The
latter he enjoyed writing as well as reading, and as often as not a
few lines about his love for her confirmed that it was all happening
and she was not day-dreaming.

Diana's memorabilia were confined to one small section of
shelving. There she placed her early film books and the annuals
which she had collected when she first began dreaming of a big
Hollywood mansion equipped with cream telephone and
swimming pool. With them too was a large red-covered book with
gold lettering called *Hollywood Album*, in which she featured
photographs of such as Ginger Rogers, Rock Hudson, Burt
Lancaster, and Shirley Maclaine. Others showed her at home in
Hollywood. On the shelf next to this stood the *Daily Mirror* album
Donald Zec on This is Show Business.

In this book he had called Miss Dors, 'The Bust of
Billingshurst':

'When this peek-a-boo blonde with the jam tart lips finally

rings down the curtains on her vital statistics, I can see no one to slip into her peep-toe shoes.'

Well, that day had come – if *Three Months Gone* had not succeeded in marking the watershed, then her increased measurements, especially the thickened waistline and double chin, did.

She said: "When you have done a life time's cheese cake, the status you get from a 'well-done' kiss from Olivier is really something. My only hope is that people will go on taking me a little more seriously. It would be worth getting really fat for that!"

11

A CLOUD ON THE HORIZON

Sundays were always home days for the Lakes. While Diana spent the morning in the kitchen preparing lunch, which was generally good old-fashioned roast beef and Yorkshire pudding, her other half would pop out to his local for a pre-prandial drink.

This, too, was the routine when they had company. After lunch there would be backgammon or a game of tennis. At opening time Alan would lead his guests back to the Red Lion, while Diana entertained the ladies.

Such was the routine on Sunday July 13 1970. The visitors for the day were pop star 'Leapy Lee' Graham and his wife Mary, with whom Diana had been friends since her Troy Dante days. Leapy, who was now very successful, following his hit record 'Little Arrows', owned a house nearby and he and Alan had become good pals. They had a similar sense of humour, enjoyed a good laugh and had a drink and a game of darts together at their local.

There was one difference on this day, though. Alan and Leapy became involved in a brawl at the Red Lion. Both men were too drunk to give their wives an explanation when they arrived home, having been treated at hospital for minor injuries. Later, the police arrived at the Manor and the pair were taken to Windsor Police Station, where they were detained for one hour. There was going to be a court case.

Diana's main worry was that, having persuaded Dickie to let Mark and Gary visit, the publicity engendered by the pub incident might make him change his mind. Everything went to plan, however, and the boys arrived with Amy. Although Alan had to appear before a Magistrate's Court, the boys seemed to remain oblivious to it all.

All that year the Lakes had been inundated with offers of work. Diana had managed to fit in the film *Deep End* during the run of *Three Months Gone*. It was a part similar to that in the play. This time she was a voluptuous, buxom attendant in a London municipal swimming bath, hugging young John Moulder Brown to her ample bosom. There was a television play too and, as a light relief from drama, a guest appearance on the Tommy Cooper Show for ITV.

In the offing now was a six-week episoder for Yorkshire Television called 'Queenie's Castle'. This was especially written for Diana by Keith Waterhouse and Willis Hall. Alan, too, was to have a starring role.

The weeks with the boys were happy ones. They did not want to go back to America when the moment arrived. Their consolation this time, though, was that mum and Alan would be able to follow them within a week or two for a much needed holiday.

This holiday in America did much to lift the gloom of Alan's forthcoming court appearance. The case was due to be held on October 16 at Reading Assize Court. They got back in good time, enabling Alan to have final briefings with his lawyer. To speed up proceedings their barristers advised both Alan and Leapy to plead guilty to the charge. Alan thought this a safe bet:

"I had no 'form' except a thirty-shilling fine for being drunk and disorderly at RADA."

The court heard that the two men were playing darts with other customers when Lake bought a round of drinks for 15s 0d. The relief manager of the hotel then said:

"I will take another 3 shillings for the Moussec you had yesterday."

Mr Michael Talbot, prosecuting, said there was a row, Lake claiming that the drink had been on the house. Leapy Lee Graham then threw a glass of beer over the manager and the fight began. Other customers joined in, and the brawl moved outside as bottles were thrown and furniture was kicked over. Mr Talbot told the court that witnesses said Lake produced 'a flick knife, long and thin, with a sharp point', and gave it to Graham. Graham rushed at the manager, Mr Anthony Stack, and lunged at his stomach. Mr Stack stepped sideways and was stabbed in the arm by Graham. He later had eighteen stitches in hospital.

Mr Simon Brown, defending Alan, said he had placed his whole career in jeopardy. He added:

"A term of imprisonment would spell doom on a career so painstakingly built up and so promising as it stands today."

Mr Kenneth Jones QC for Graham, said:

"He had been hit on the head and involved in a fierce mêlée, and at that moment a knife was put in his hands. The result was inevitable."

The men, who pleaded guilty to malicious wounding and causing damage, denied causing grievous bodily harm, and this was accepted by the prosecution. Neither man had any previous convictions, but Mr Justice Everleigh told them:

"Crimes of violence are all too prevalent today. It must not be thought that anyone can indulge in this sort of behaviour without being sent to prison."

The judge then sentenced Lee Graham to three years in gaol, and Alan Lake to eighteen months. They were also given nine-month sentences to be served concurrently, for smashing six windows, twelve glasses, a chair, and a garden umbrella at the Red Lion Hotel.

Alan could hardly believe what was happening to him. Later, he recalled:

"When the judge said, 'You will go to prison for eighteen months', I stood there waiting for him to add 'the sentence will be suspended'. But the words didn't come."

Like everyone else, Diana had been optimistic about the outcome. Now she leant forward, head in hands, and burst into tears. She was still shaking when a policewoman led her down to the cells to see her husband. They were given just three minutes together.

On her arrival home the first thing the actress did was phone Stoke-on-Trent, where Jason was being looked after by her in-laws.

There was nothing else for her but to pack her bags and travel up to Leeds by herself for the first day's filming of 'Queenie's Castle'. It was the worst journey she had ever had to make, haunted all the way by fears for Alan; how would he cope when the other prisoners learnt he was the husband of the country's only sex-symbol? She felt sure he would be teased mercilessly.

As it happened Alan was treated fairly by the other prisoners – after, that is, he smacked in the mouth one smart-alec who had for three days continually sung 'Stay by me Diana'!

In 'Queenies Castle', Diana, getting somewhat typecast, played a blowsy mother of three teenage sons who share a council flat with her brother-in-law. This part was to have been played by Alan, but was now taken over by Tony Caunter. The situation was difficult for Caunter too, but Diana had nothing but praise for his understanding:

"Everyone's been a brick and so nice, especially Tony. But, of course, it's not the same as it would have been with Alan."

Diana also travelled to Stoke-on-Trent to do what she could to comfort Alan's parents. In between takes she wrote long letters to her husband, as often as three times a week. And she carried a calendar in her handbag, ticking off each day.

Christmas 1970 saw Alan transferred to Verne Prison, on wind-swept Portland Bill, in Dorset. Back home at Orchard Manor, Diana, alone but for baby Jason and his nanny, was utterly despondent. It was the most wretched Yuletide she had ever experienced. As midnight Christmas Eve approached, she put on her coat and went to the village church. There she sat through the Midnight Service, wondering what had happened to all the happiness that had surrounded Jason's baptism.

There was one ray of hope for the new year of 1971, and that was that the appeal judges might reduce the entertainers' prison sentences. Laurence Olivier had taken it upon himself to marshall together numbers of letters and testimonials regarding Alan's character in an effort to sway them. The appeal was heard on January 21. Olivier's efforts, though, were to no avail.

Alan was naturally despondent. Nevertheless, he accepted the judgment and Diana even began to feel cheerful after her monthly visits. Her husband was looking much more fit and healthy, due in no small measure to the fact that he was being prevented from regular heavy drinking.

He spoke of the shows he had arranged for the inmates, and about members of the Women's Institute who came along to watch his prison productions.

"I think a prison waiting room is the saddest place in the world," Diana said in an interview. "I am alright because I go down in my Rolls. But some wives struggle along with three or four children and no transport.

"Alan tells me many of the prisoners receive 'Dear John' letters ending their marriages. No wonder men like that drop right out of the world. They are shattered."

Diana got stuck into her work. She had a house to maintain, back tax to pay, and she also wanted to put some money by so that Alan would have a surprise to welcome him home. In February 1971, she went off to Spain to film *Hannie Caulder* with Ernest Borgnine and Raquel Welch, and then threw herself into cabaret work. There were plans too for a film in Germany, and for a television play, *A Taste of Honey*.

Alan, though, was to be restored to her earlier than expected for, by his behaviour in prison, he had earned a six-month remission and was released on October 16, exactly a year after he was sentenced.

Diana did not meet Alan as he walked out of prison at 7.00 am on the morning of October 16 1971. Instead, she sent her chauffeur-driven Rolls Royce to pick him up and take him to a friend's small terraced house in nearby Weymouth. Before he was allowed in the car, however, the press had to have his first reactions.

"It's marvellous to be free again. The first thing I want to do is see Diana and hold her in my arms. Then I'd like a really good breakfast...without porridge!"

As the Rolls drove off, the reporters kept at a discreet distance, but they were on hand to witness the reunion. Diana waited just inside the front door as her husband ran down the path and into the house to give her a long kiss. Then they closed the door, and the curtains in the front room were drawn as they toasted their future with a pre-breakfast bottle of champagne.

A banner over the high gates of Orchard Manor read 'Welcome Home Alan'. And there inside waiting to greet him were his parents, Cyril and Millicent, with little Jason in the arms of his nanny. Diana's homecoming present was £6,000 in bank notes, which she had worked non-stop to save especially for him. The next day, during a champagne reception attended by over one hundred friends, Diana had another surprise in store for her husband. She presented him with a magnificent seventeen-hand grey mare. Her name was Sapphire. Alan was overcome with emotion at yet another act of love.

"Oh, don't forget, darling," said Diana, "you have to be at the Old Bailey on Monday...it's handcuffs for you again!"

Alan's appointment, however, was to appear in a film the BBC were making of 'Dixon of Dock Green'. His part was that of a lodger in a boarding house – the landlady was Diana Dors!

12

A MOMENT OF ILLUMINATION

On February 20 1972, Alan left Orchard Manor for his regular morning ride in nearby Windsor Great Park. On his way back to the stables he came through some trees, and found his path blocked by one that had partly fallen. A huge bough stuck up from the ground like some giant arm. Expert horseman that he was, he knew that it would be impossible to jump it. So he pushed Sapphire's and his own head down low and tried to steer the animal between stump and bough. They did not make it and Alan's back took the full impact. He was wrenched from the horse.

His condition was made worse by well-intentioned riders who in ignorance not only had him on his feet, but made him walk. By the time Diana reached the hospital, where her husband had been taken by ambulance, she found him in a side ward reserved for the dying.

The doctors told her that the damage was irreparable: the patient had broken his back in two places, plus six ribs. It was most unlikely he would last the night out and even if he did live, he would certainly be paralysed.

She stayed by his bed all night long, hoping that the slightest groan or movement would mean that he was regaining consciousness. She talked aloud and then in whispers, and she prayed to a God she was not sure existed.

At daybreak Alan opened his eyes, turned them with difficulty in his wife's direction, smiled, then grimaced as the pain suddenly enveloped him.

"I made it," he whispered. "I made it...darling, I heard them saying, 'Put him in a side ward, then when he pops off he won't disturb the other patients'. From then on, I willed myself back to consciousness."

But Alan was not sure he had opted for the better alternative, as the pain of broken bones, stretched muscles and torn sinews ate into his being. The three-hourly morphine injections eased the pain for just half-an-hour at a time. And so it continued, even after his transfer to Ashford Hospital, in Middlesex, where he was put on traction.

Alan devised his own methods of coping with it, however, as his friends smuggled in small hip flasks of whisky and brandy. Nothing gave him greater pleasure than a crate of champagne sent in by the cast and crew of *Innocent Bystanders*, the film he was due to start shortly in Spain with Orson Welles and Stanley Baker.

It was not long before he confounded the doctors, who had said he would never again stand, let alone walk, by taking a few steps around his bed. Contrary to all expectations, in a matter of just three weeks, Alan's request to go home was granted.

"Doctor," he said as he left, "It won't be long before I'm riding again in Windsor Great Park."

Alan was much happier in the environment he loved, though he was not to see as much of his wife as he wished. At the crack of dawn she would slide out of bed as gently and quietly as she could, so as not to waken her husband, then off to work. So it was the company of baby Jason, now able to toddle and almost hold a little conversation, and a new young nanny, Miss Gwen Daley, that Alan became used to.

He read nursery rhymes to his son in a voice and intonation which would be the envy of many a father. Always a bit of a scribbler, he also spent time writing poetry, an excellent form of therapy.

He enjoyed the company of the young students attached to the religious order of the Verona Fathers, so named after the city in which they were founded. They were constant visitors. The property of the Fathers adjoined Orchard Manor at the bottom of the garden, and it was by way of a little pathway that Miss Daley made her way each Sunday to attend Mass.

Of course, the students knew her and where she worked, which gave them a ready excuse to go across to Orchard Manor in the hopes of meeting its illustrious incumbents, which they did. They had seen Alan in hospital too, and Fr Fontanari, one of the priests, had gone over to Ashford when he was on traction.

During his close shave with death, when the actor had had to fight so hard to regain consciousness, his thoughts had turned to God. Was there a hereafter? Did life have a purpose? Did God exist? In the twilight zone of semi-consciousness Alan experienced no fear, but a real sense of the supernatural. It made him seek the answers to life, to posit the existence of God. Later, back at Orchard Manor, he seemed to sense some of the answers in the presence of these young men, prepared to give up so many of the things in life he had come to regard as necessities, in order to go as missionaries to Africa. Not only did they keep him company, but they helped to get him on his feet again. They had a happiness, a 'something' he himself had not, and he was anxious to share it. So did Miss Daley, who each time she left the house for church would say, "I'll pray for you today as I always do."

Long before the summer air dispelled the chill of spring, Alan was on horseback again. It was not just in Windsor Great Park this time, but on location for his starring role in *Zappers – Blade of Vengeance*.

Diana could not have been more pleased with her husband's progress, and she was overjoyed too, that he, like her, was waking to an early call.

The lady of the house was working again with old chum Lionel Jeffries. This time Lionel was directing *The Amazing Mr Blunden*. Aimed at the family market, he was endeavouring to follow up his very successful directorial début with *The Railway Children*, made in 1970. Diana played Mrs Wickens, a wicked, conniving wart-nosed woman from the past, whose dastardly plot to do away with two innocent children is foiled by Laurence Naismith and Lynn Frederick, the latter playing in her first film. Diana thoroughly enjoyed the whole production. Her part was the biggest for a long time and it gave her a great deal of satisfaction.

Her next assignment was 'All Our Saturdays', a follow-up to 'Queenie's Castle'. Once again she was in the Leeds Television studios.

The actress had no complaints about her busy life except for wanting a good holiday, or, more particularly, that delayed honeymoon they had always promised themselves, but which because of so many traumas they had been unable to take.

In August an opportunity presented itself when Alan finished an episode of 'Villians' for ITV. Diana decided on Venice and Rome.

During their stay in Venice, they decided to do what all honeymooners do – be serenaded on the Grand Canal by a gondolier. This time, Diana was fully clad, and there was no cavalcade of cameramen forming a flotilla around her. Alan was smartly dressed, too, and wearing his 'honeymoon' present, a two-thousand-pound watch.

As he went down the steps he slipped, lost his footing, knocked his head hard on the side of the gondola and ended up in the canal. Dragged out by the Gondolier, he finally emerged, cut, bleeding, and covered from head to toe in mud. The two-thousand-pound watch was a complete write-off.

Back home again, Alan began to feel the effects of his tumble into the canal; his back began to play up again. He tried to deaden the pain with whisky and brandy, and drank more and more out of the sheer boredom and frustration that comes from having nothing to do.

Diana, on the other hand, had hardly a moment to herself. In the autumn, she started on a horror film with David Warner and Nyree Dawn Porter, called *From Beyond the Grave*, and then at the beginning of 1973 there was *Steptoe and Son Ride Again*, and another horror entitled *Theatre of Blood*.

Invariably, when Diana returned home from a gruelling day at the studio, she found Alan drunk. This led to bitter arguments, and in one case alarm and panic, when she found Alan in a state of hallucination, his eyes glazed and staring, believing himself to be a soldier in the trenches of France in the First World War. When he came round next day he did not remember a thing. Diana had already left for the studio, and Miss Daley was left to see to him. And this she began to do regularly.

One day after a bad drinking bout, she said to her employer:

"Mr Lake, why don't you pop over to my church sometime, and sit there quietly? It might help you."

Taking her advice, he did visit the small Church of the Sacred Heart. From then on the Community of the Verona Fathers were always to know when Alan was working and when not. So much a part of his life had those visits become, that even without the sanction of the Church itself he began to claim the Catholic religion as his own and he did all he could to persuade his loved ones to do the same. Vilma, Alan's sister, was very much bemused by it all:

"Having accepted the faith himself, he wanted Diana, he wanted me, he wanted my mother, all of us to change. He'd discovered this faith, hadn't he? He went completely over the top, wanting us all to convert."

Diana did not know what to make of it, but as far as she was concerned, if it was going to help him with his drinking problem, then it was alright by her.

Down in the village shopping one day, Diana bumped into a clergyman whom she recognised as being from the church next door. She smiled at him and, in her usual outspoken way, said:

"Good morning. I wonder, are you the one who gives my little Jason a lift from the nursery school?" Diana smiled at the five-foot-nothing dark haired priest.

"Yes, I am." Fr Theodore Fontanari smiled back and ran his fingers through three-year-old Jason's blonde hair.

"Well, I'm very grateful to you, sir. Our nanny told me about it."

"Ah, yes," Fr Fontanari nodded.

"One day I'd like to come and see your church." Diana Lake raised her finely arched eyebrows.

"Of course you can. I would be delighted to show you round myself."

The priest's pronounced but lyrical accent reflected the warmth of his nature. Then his eyes twinkled, "But Madam, I'm not a sir, I'm a Father, Father Fontanari."

Diana laughed too, "Oh, I am sorry, Father... and I *will* come and see you soon. Thank you again for looking after Jason."

Fr Theodiore Fontanari waved goodbye as mother and son continued on their way. Although the priest had visited Alan Lake when he was at Ashford Hospital, it was the first time he had met his wife, and he was pleasantly taken aback by the warmth and graciousness of the star he had been told was once known as Britain's scarlet woman!

"Very much to my surprise," Fr Theo said, "Diana turned up the following Sunday looking a bit sheepish and rather conspicuous. She had a scarf over her head covering that famous platinum blonde hair. She didn't wear any make-up and sat at the very back of the church. The following Sunday she came again. This time, Alan, her husband, was with her. He was wearing riding breeches. After that they came regularly each Sunday. One day I said to Alan, 'I understand from your wife that you have a lovely singing voice. Why don't you sing in the choir?' And that's what he did... he had a beautiful voice."

Attending church was more of a novel experience for Diana than it was for Alan. Apart from the occasional Christmas vigil, the only connection she had had with church in her adult life was to be on the receiving end of a condemnation from the Archbishop of Canterbury.

Diana had been christened in the Church of England but her only recollection of ever having gone to church was to ogle a choir boy she fancied. When interest in him waned, so did her attendance.

In fact, the young Diana had always been suspicious of

church-going people. To her, attending church was the habit of
the snobbish and boringly respectable. It epitomised for her the
actions of the narrow-minded, hypocritical community of the
middle-classes in which she was brought up. Furthermore, she
hated Sunday with its closed shops, routine chatter around the
family table, and nothing to do!

As for Roman Catholics, there was nothing at all to endear
them to her. As a young starlet in Hollywood, she attracted the
wrath of the very staid Woman's Catholic Guild of America for
having an affair with a married man. She said of Catholics:

"I felt they were a sanctimonious lot who preached gloom,
practised confessing their sins, but never did anything about
putting them right."

The impact made by the Roman Catholic Church on her
husband, however, made her think. She wanted to be completely
one with her husband in everything, and so began to wonder
whether maybe there was something in Christianity after all.

Diana persisted in attending church with her husband and
singing in the choir. Often they were spotted by a member of the
community, when there were no services taking place, sitting side
by side in the front pew holding hands. The church was built so
that for most of the day the rays of the sun shone in from long
rectangular strips of tinted glass windows partitioning the green
walls of the church.

"The peace and the tranquility of the church was unlike
anything we'd experienced in our lives. In the end it was this,"
Diana told her friends, "that persuaded us both to try and become
Catholics. Alan was already a favourite with the priests and the
little church's congregation, and it just made sense to come and
have a go."

An opportunity was to present itself, though it was not to
take the form Diana would have chosen. While appearing in
cabaret at Wakefield in 1973, she broke her ankle tripping over a
high step. An operation was performed, placing a pin in her leg.
For three months she lay helpless at home, very much as her

husband had done earlier in 1972.

As soon as he heard of Mrs Lake's indisposition Fr
Fontanari asked one of the nuns at the nearby Marist Convent to
go and see her to ask if she would like to see a priest. When the
reply came back in the affirmative, Fr Theo went himself.

"Oh, Father, how delighted I am to see you." She hugged
and kissed him from her wheelchair. "You know, Father, I've
been thinking of joining your Church, of becoming a real
Christian."

"Well, Diana," said the priest, "we prayed for you at
church and everybody wishes you a speedy recovery. The people
of the parish remember seeing you."

Diana smiled back broadly, "Oh, Father, I'd love to come
to your church again, but I can't the way I am. D'you know, the
first time I entered your church it seemed that the hand of an angel
swept by my cheek, stroking my face — and something heavenly
came over me — and I received a great gift of peace." It was a
feeling of tremendous spiritual intensity which the star could
never totally explain.

Alan had to wheel her down the long drive that led from her
home, then along the main road to the church. But soon a short cut
was devised through the back of both the church's property and
Orchard Manor. Strong planks were placed over a ditch that
separated them. Overcoming her initial embarrassment at being
in a wheelchair, she no longer stayed at the back, but had her
wheelchair placed at the top of the aisle.

Becoming a Catholic for Diana was not going to be the
simple matter she thought. Initially, the Church was very
suspicious of her motives and did all they could to dissuade her.
They knew about her past and that her second marriage had
ended in divorce. She had, however, a very strong ally in Fr
Fontanari. He knew that Mr and Mrs Lake's desire to become
Catholics was no passing whim. Furthermore, they loved one
another deeply and had confounded those who said their marriage
would last only a few weeks, by staying together for six years.

Father Fontanari's opinion prevailed in the end, and upon his recommendation, Fr Simon,the Parish Priest of Englefield Green, under whose jurisdiction the couple came, took them for instruction.

"His English," laughed Fr Fontanari, "is much better than mine. You'll be able to understand all he has to say!"

Even then it took at least a year before the authorities cleared the way for Diana's entry into the Church.

"It was very hard for her," said Alan's sister, Vilma, "I really admired her for it. She had to undergo a lot of counselling, and for a long time too, and she stuck with it."

So in 1974 the way to entering the Church was eventually opened. Firstly, Fr Simon was satisfied that husband and wife had the gift of faith, and secondly the Church ruled that Diana's marriage to Dickie Dawson did not constitute the proper conditions of a true commitment.

Diana and Alan asked Lionel Jefferies and his wife Eileen to sponsor them. They had been friends for years, Lionel and Diana having recently worked together on *The Amazing Mr Blunden*.

When they were received into the Church it was suggested that they have a blessing on their marriage. Both were delighted and readily agreed. Alan was especially happy.

"He always wanted a church wedding," his sister explained. "Alan loved the church at Bagnall, which is not far from our village of Milton. It was old and had so much history and character. Ken and I were married there and, of course, he would have liked to be married there too. But Diana had been divorced, so they settled for Caxton Hall. But I know Alan always felt that it wasn't a proper wedding."

As this was going to be a truly auspicious occasion for Diana and Alan, they asked if they could make their vows in the church where it all happened, and which they knew and loved so well. And it was in the Church of the Sacred Heart that the wedding was conducted.

"I was there once more," Fr Theo recalls. "Half-way through their wedding vows, at the words, 'till death do us part', Diana was so overwhelmed that she broke down and started crying. Father Simon took hold of her lovely long hair and gently wiped away her tears, just as Jesus did Mary Magdalen!"

It was a very emotional moment for both Alan and Diana, who knew in their hearts that now their marriage was for life.

Diana Dors and Ty Hardin in a scene from the "circus thriller"
Berserk **filmed in Britain in 1967 with Joan Crawford co-starring.**
Matilda, a performer in The Great Rivers Circus, and its "sex
bomb", tries to seduce Frank Hawking, the circus aerialist, in his
caravan.

Alan Lake

Family photo of wedding in 1968. L to R Vilma — Her son, Mark — Cyril Lake — Alan — Diana — Little Glyn Thursfield — Millicent Lake — Ken Thursfield.

Diana Dors as the evil Mrs Wickens in *The Amazing Mr Blunden* (1972).

**Diana Dors and Alan Lake in hospital (November 1974). A cheerful
Diana, 43, sits up in bed as she gets a visit from her husband, Alan, in
the London hospital where she is recovering from meningitis.**

Diana Dors leaves the Chertsey Court with her son Gary in October 1979.

Alan, Diana and Jason.

Diana and Alan are received into the Catholic Church. L to R Fr Fontanari — Diana — Alan — Fr Simon.

Posing for a publicity shot for what turned out to be her very last film, *Steaming*, Diana still bravely smiles at the camera shortly before her death in 1984.

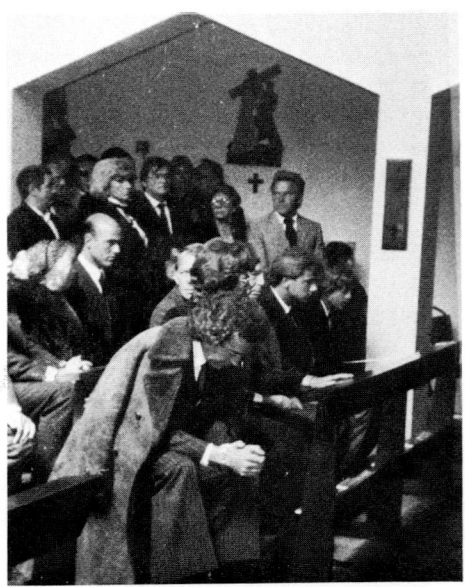

Alan Lake in mournful mood as he listens to his wife's funeral service. He was to follow her into death soon enough.

Next to each other — "only a whisper away" — lie the late Diana Dors and her third husband, Alan Lake. Flowers always seem to appear on their graves as fans and loved ones help to keep their memory alive. Alan could not go on living without his beloved Diana.

13

A NATIONAL INSTITUTION

Soon after her reception into the Catholic Church, Diana received news of the death of Kathleen Evans. Auntie Kit had been living in the family home in Marlborough Road since the death of Bert Fluck, and her letters had kept the niece in touch with her home town. On the trip to sell the property and to see to the Fluck family affairs, she could not help noticing how rapidly Swindon was expanding, and how already it had lost some of the stuffiness and insularity of her younger days.

"I suppose in my way I have appeared rather nasty about Swindon," she said, "but it is home to me. It has a lot of happy memories. I was pleased to get away years ago because I was full of ambition.

"I think Swindon would not bring itself to admit it had fostered a star – and a controversial one at that. They thought I would come back here and amount to nothing. You always find jealousy and lack of recognition in your own home town. I have seen it happen to other people in all parts of the world. They think, 'You are the same, so why should you be looked on as anything different?'. I think that's the reason."

When she landed the role of Jocasta in *Oedipus Tyrannus* at the prestigious Chichester Festival Theatre, the people of Swindon were first to hear of it, though. The role of Queen Jocasta, a mythical matriarchal ruler, who marries her son Oedipus after he has murdered his father, was her most challenging yet, and Diana was very excited about it when approached by director Keith Michell in February of 1974. I was certainly far removed from *What the Butler Saw*, *The Amorous Milkman*, *Bedtime with Rosie*, and *Three for All*, her bit part offerings for the rest of the year! Some critics labelled it as the most bizarre piece of casting they had come across; one compared it to Lord Olivier being chosen to play 'Peanuts'!

During rehearsals Diana worked hard, determined to wipe the grin off the faces of her critics. Keith Michell, who had chosen himself to play opposite her as Oedipus, and who had put his own reputation on the line in choosing her, worked alongside the former sex-symbol, encouraging and supporting her, as did husband Alan.

Alan was pleased to coach and offer advice. He did all in his power to help Diana, and as opening night approached he was far more nervous than she.

The performance, on July 8 1974, was a triumph for Diana. When the curtains finally fell the applause for her was louder than for any other member of a distinguished cast. The critics, too, were generally unanimous in praise for Diana Dors. One described her as 'splendid', another wrote that 'She brings genuine humanity into the production'.

When the Chichester Festival ended and Diana had completed 'Nurse Will Make It Better', a television drama, she was able to settle down to a normal life with Alan and Jason, now five years old. They were looking forward to celebrating their sixth wedding anniversary. On November 23, Diana, never a one to complain of feeling poorly, did so to Miss Pat Hughes, Jason's Nanny of the time.

"After tea, Mrs. Lake complained of headaches and aching all over. She had an aspirin and went to bed early," remembers Miss Hughes.

The following morning she felt just as ill and stayed in bed believing it to be flu. About lunchtime Alan heard his wife call out. Racing upstairs he found her threshing around in the bed holding her head and screaming in anguish. At 2pm she was on her way to the London National Hospital for Neurological Research, in Bloomsbury. She went into a coma. Later, meningitis was diagnosed.

That evening the doctors held out little hope. After a

six-hour vigil by her bedside a very tearful Alan Lake walked across the road to a pub. He told anxious reporters who followed him there:

"The doctors said we will know the worst within twelve hours. I'm completely knocked sideways. Di has never had a day's illness in her life.

"All I know is, she has been a great fighter all her life and I know that she is fighting now."

As Alan left to return to the hospital all the customers raised their glasses to her health. One said, "You go back there and tell her that we are all rooting for her. She is one of the all-time great birds."

And fight that 'great bird' did. She forced herself to consciousness at about midnight, squeezed Alan's hand and said, "Hello, darling."

The doctor's opinion as to her chances changed. They told Alan she would make it.

The next few days in hospital there were uncountable bouquets and baskets of flowers. She received calls from Hollywood from Joan Crawford and Myrna Loy, wishing in her heart of hearts that they had been instead from Gary and Mark.

"Look, Alan." She picked out some of the hundreds of letters she had received.

'We're praying for you, Di, you can't go. Life just wouldn't be the same without you.'

'Keep fighting,' wrote another, 'you're part of Britain, part of our bricks and mortar.'

'D'you hear that, Alan. I'm a National Institution,' she smiled.

"I know, darling. Fancy me having to share you with the whole nation!"

"Do you know what's been brought home to me these last few days?" she said. "I always believed that most people thought of me as a sex-symbol, but, you know, it seems I'm much more than that!"

Diana's recovery from meningitis had bordered on the miraculous, but the the doctors still feared to tell Alan there and then about the debilities associated with meningitis, such as deafness, blindness or paralysis.

Remarkably, her recovery was total.

Within seven weeks, Diana was back rehearsing Edgar Wallace's play *Murder Mistaken*, which was to run at Harrogate in the new year. Her real reason for accepting this role so soon was that it offered work for Alan, who was having a lean spell. There was a good, demanding role for the lead male to absorb his interest.

Although the Lakes were well conditioned to shocks and traumas, they were quite unprepared for the discovery during Diana's period of recuperation that she was pregnant.

"You see, for three-and-a-half years I had taken no precautions. I am forty-four this year, and thought I must have reached the age when I could no longer bear children."

After the initial shock, both Alan and Diana were thrilled. The doctors, however, had other ideas. The pregnancy should be terminated. Diana's poor health and age were against her. A date was set for an abortion. This put a great strain on Diana morally, for she knew the Church's teaching on the matter. For two weeks she wavered between the consistent advice of her doctors and the dictates of her conscience. Then, while she and Alan were at Brighton, she broke down in tears:

"Darling, it's no good, I can't go through with an abortion."

Alan's mum, Millicent, was not so happy about the decision. She told her son straight:

"Well, you'll have to mend your ways for a start off."

The Lakes had a wonderful summer together, preparing for their baby. The nanny had left, and Diana loved being able to care for her boy herself. All went well with the pregnancy and they looked forward to the arrival of the new Lake.

Then, one day, sitting side by side with her husband in the

drawing room, Diana suddenly felt, as she put it, "as if the cold hand of death had passed through me". She began shaking and sobbed uncontrollably. Alan hastily fetched blankets and when she was wrapped up warmly, calmed her down.

At her usual check-up a few days later, the doctors could not hear the baby's heartbeat. Then came a period of limbo, when Alan was being a tower of strength for his wife. Before the doctors could determine whether the baby was alive or dead, Diana went into labour, and the local doctor arranged for her to travel by ambulance to Westminster Hospital. The baby arrived prematurely. It was still-born. Alan stayed at her side throughout the night and the next day to cosset and cuddle until the flow of tears stopped. The infant had been a boy, the spitting image of the new-born Jason.

14

THE DEVIL'S BREW

Every marriage has its most difficult phase, and now Alan and Diana were entering theirs. Their previous traumas – broken legs and backs, prison sentences and meningitis – had served only to bring the couple closer together, but at the same time they had turned a blind eye to a more basic disorder in their relationship, which stemmed from Alan's drinking.

This problem now came to a head, because of the loss of their baby. Alan was not able to cope with it as Diana had been able to do. He had become hysterical in the hospital itself, and, having been abstemious during the pregnancy, suddenly found himself ricocheting from pub to pub, and from bar to bar, in order to drown his sorrows.

Right from the very beginning of their marriage, Diana accepted that her husband was a heavy drinker. When they first met on the set of 'The Inquisitors', she was aware that Alan liked to start work with a dram or two. Then she got used to his inviting friends home for a 'quick' drink, which lasted until the early hours of the morning. Busy with work, Diana always excused herself and retired early to bed. In the morning, she made no comment about the empty beer cans, filled ashtrays, broken glasses and upturned furniture. She was rather philosophical about it all.

"You can't always have things your own way. Besides, how could you be angry with a man you loved so much? He puts up with my faults, so I must put up with his."

Diana's tolerance sprang from her experience of a show-business world where heavy drinking was far from uncommon. She knew well all the stresses and strains, the tensions during a rehearsal as well as a performance, and she had often seen actors and actresses have a tipple before going on stage or appearing in front of the camera. She was only too aware that when she left the security of LAMDA and started mixing with the in-crowd, she could equally well have become hooked, were it not for the fact that drinking made her violently ill. If one had a weakness for alcohol, then the acting profession would certainly exploit it, as it had Alan, who happened to be more vulnerable than most.

Alan was basically a very shy and retiring person, whose early life revolved around his mother and sister.

"I'm nine years older than Alan," said Vilma, "so I was a mum to him as well as my own mother, and he needed all our love. Alan was born at a very difficult time, you see. It was World War II. My mother had to go out to work, because at the time, if you didn't, then you always had someone billetted on you, an airman or something. We went through all that. I was very protective of him.

"In fact, Alan was always a home-loving boy. He very rarely went out. He was just content to stay at home with us."

It was somewhere around the age of fifteen that Alan had his first drink. It was then that he discovered a new and brasher self.

Alan remembered:

"I would leave my parents' respectable little house, and go and meet my mates. We would secretly open a few bottles, then I would emerge as The Baron, Teddy Boy leader of the local gang."

When Alan left Milton for RADA it was a tremendous wrench. His parents too, could hardly believe that their lad was leaving the nest.

"Boys from his background in Stoke-on-Trent," said his sister, "just didn't leave home. You can imagine what a shock it was when he won the scholarship to RADA and actually decided to up and out, and to leave home to go into acting."

In the 1950s, young men of working-class backgrounds very rarely, if ever, left the industrial provinces of the North. They went to the factory or office, paid their mums their keep, went to the pub, cinema or local dance hall, married a girl from down the street and went to live with mum-in-law.

Some rebelled against the system with its repression and lack of opportunity, and this ushered in the era of the 'angry young man' at the tail end of the 'fifties. From the moment Alan was told to rid himself of his 'awful' potteries accent, he began his fight against the system.

In those early days in London, he was still very much a fish out of water, and for all his bravado, a rather gullible seventeen-year-old.

"When I came from Stoke-on-Trent to go to RADA I thought London was fantastic – the concrete and the traffic and the rush everywhere, the West End and all that, the club bit, being up all night, living with the pack sort of thing."

Unsure of himself, he was easily led, and thought that downing pints of beer, often as many as 14 or 15 a night, was the best proof that he had come of age. It was a wild, irresponsible and even decadent time for the son of a Stoke-on-Trent glazier, as he tried to conform to his own image of a budding young actor.

Cyril and Millicent were very generous in their support, little dreaming of what he got up to away from RADA. But even their financial contributions and his scholarship could not keep up with his daily round. Making the most of a good voice, Alan began to earn money for his pints and pies, by learning Irish ballads and singing them with an accent and a sob in his voice in Irish pubs in Soho.

After Alan left RADA, repertory took him up and down the country. He appeared in such favourites as *Sailor Beware*, and *When we are Married*. Because his meagre wage did not cover his needs, Alan became adept at 'The Mumble', a favourite trick to keep the actor in drinks. The idea was that he would keep his make-up on and, while waiting to be served in the theatre bar or the pub next door, ask a member of the audience how they had enjoyed the play. Flattered at being asked, a hand would go straight into the pocket and the night's free drinking was under way!

Right from the early days of their meeting, Diana was well

aware of Alan's insecurity and that the bravado drink gave him was only a cover-up for his inhibitions and fears. She knew too, that Alan found in drink all the confidence he needed to survive in a highly competitve show-biz world, and initially, too, to relate to women. She said:

"By speaking to women in a rather shocking manner, as he often did, he was using such outrageous behaviour to protect himself in case they hurt him.

"There had been one girl with whom, while a young actor in rep, he fell in love," said Diana. "Tragically, she died of cancer, though a baby girl was born of another relationship a year or so before we met. After that he devoted all his interest and time to acting, treating all females with a certain contempt. This, contrarily but inevitably, made him more interesting to the opposite sex!"

In her naïveté, Diana considered her husband just a heavy drinker. Furthermore, Alan's inconsistent behaviour was to her no different from Hamilton's and, indeed, that of most of the other men she had had dealings with. She was slow to see that her husband was becoming more and more dependent on the drink.

Because she was often away, she missed some of Alan's worst benders but, more importantly, her absences meant that time hung heavily on his hands, causing him to drink more. Unfortunately, the Sacred Heart Church, which had acted as a novitiate for students, closed down that part of its work, and the young men who used to keep Alan company were now at the Missionary Institute at Mill Hill, London.

The result of all this was that the actor became edgy and depressed. He also gradually came to resent the success his wife was experiencing in her rejuvenated career. Diana understood. She had seen it before in Dickie Dawson. Alan likewise resented being called 'Mr Dors', or being introduced as Diana Dors's husband. In many ways Alan felt this more acutely; he was a very good actor in his own right, and at the time he met Diana, had been tipped to reach the heights. The birth of his still-born son was the final blow.

Diana noticed the drinking bouts becoming more regular, and decided to seek professional help. Told that her husband was an alcoholic, Diana left no stone unturned in her search for a cure. She made Alan accept the fact that he needed special treatment, and, after much resistance and many heated arguments, Alan finally agreed to go to hospital, to St Andrews in Northampton, the Alcohol Treatment Unit.

When he came out, the couple experienced a period of bliss with Alan at his wittiest best and no longer incoherent and maudlin.

The news that his mother had cancer, however, caused a relapse during the summer of 1976. Diana now had to endure his appearances in court on drunk and disorderly charges, ejections from clubs and restaurants, and nights spent in ditches. Alan was in an alarming state, and was often downright rude to anyone who called at Orchard Manor. When he plunged into his worst bouts of drinking, which could go on for four or five days at a time, Diana and Jason would leave home for an hotel. On one occasion, when she thought she could stand it no more, they went away for a long rest at Brighton. There she received urgent news that her husband was at death's door.

"I rushed back. Alan was taken out of the house on a stretcher, completely dehydrated. I'd never seen him look so close to death since his riding accident."

Once more everything was done to help. Alan had to undergo numerous unpleasant treatments. On his release a month later, he was determined never to drink again, but the old pressures and frustrations proved too much.

Diana did not know where to turn. She had done all she could. The problem seemed insurmountable. The advice of her friends had always been the same: leave him. This she could not do

"It is up to those more fortunate," she said, "to help and understand this illness."

The trouble was, Alan could never understand that he was

an ill man, as his sister Vilma said:

"He was so much alright the day after a drinking bout, that he couldn't understand why no one was talking to him. 'What's wrong?' he asked, 'why is everyone down on me?' When we told him why, he always promised he'd never drink again."

Diana's only consolation lay with her new-found faith. She began praying for a cure for Alan and for the strength she needed to cope. She reminded her husband to do the same. Diana was in no doubt that alcohol was, as it was nicknamed, the devil's brew.

It would be necessary for Alan to go to the very depths of despair before he would admit his problem and cry out for help. She was determined to be around when that happened.

15

WALKING THE TIGHTROPE
OF AFFECTION

In view of her husband's erratic behaviour, Diana decided to send her young son to boarding school. It was a decision she loathed making. When the actress was expecting her second child, she had spent those few months at home so enjoyably with Jason, and really felt she had got to know him. It was the first time in her life that she really knew what it was like to have a son.

When Mark and Gary's mother had returned to England in 1966, her career had been very much in the doldrums. Apart from the occasional film, in which she was more likely to have a cameo role than a lead, there was only cabaret. This meant travelling from one hotel to another, living out of a suitcase. It was hardly a fit life for two boys, whom she knew were adored, loved and so well cared for by their father in the healthy climate of California.

Dickie Dawson never ever got over the acrimony of the divorce. He had remained bitter towards his ex-wife. Diana said that she was able to keep friendly with all the men in her life, even with Tommy Yeardye, who had married an ex-model and was doing very well for himself working for Vidal Sassoon, but with Dickie it was different. Dawson did little to foster any sort of worthwhile relationship between mother and sons. From 1970 to 1974 there was a cold war.

Alan's court case and imprisonment had precluded any visits the children might have liked to have made to Orchard Manor in 1971. Then there was his riding accident and months of incapacity. All this had militated against travel either way. The result was that she had heard nothing from her sons. There was never any reply to her letters or acknowledgement of her birthday or Christmas presents. In early 1974, Diana was determined to do something about it.

The star's busy work schedule meant that she could only manage a few days in America, but she was able to spend them alone with the boys, because the possessive Amy was in hospital undergoing treatment for cancer.

The first thing Diana did was to try to re-establish her relationship with them. She wanted desperately to reassure them of her love and explain the reason for her long absences.

"How come then, mum," said Mark, "if you thought so much of us, you never sent us anything at birthdays and Christmas?"

Diana's heart sank inside.

"But I did, son, I did!"

At last the mother's suspicions about those presents, and the 'thank you' letters she never received, were confirmed. She guessed that Amy, not Dickie, was responsible for this.

Because of meningitis in November of that same year, her pregnancy, and then the loss of her baby, the only chance Diana had of a return visit was in January 1976. This time Alan went with her and they took Jason too. Mark and Gary had not seen their brother for six years, and Jason did not know them at all. Since Diana's last visit both boys had grown considerably, and when this six-foot adonis with hair as long as her own stepped forward at the airport, she could hardly believe it was Mark.

There was no Amy. She had died the previous June. Now Diana hoped that relations would improve. Indeed, even Dickie was a different person. He was now a top TV host, and full of the confidence and self-respect that comes from fame and influence.

Happy and buoyant after their splendid holiday, the Lakes returned to England. Diana had made tentative arrangements to see her sons again in 1977.

"Perhaps," she suggested, "we could all come over again and go with you and your father to Hawaii," during the latter's vacation from television.

The success of David Niven's book, *The Moon's a Balloon*,

published in 1971, made many people in show business suddenly develop the literary bug. Diana had for some time nursed a secret ambition to write her life story, but her commitments did not make that possible.

The year 1977, on the other hand, proved a fallow year for the Lake family workwise. All Alan was able to get were 'voice-overs' for John Courage, Ansell's and Tetley Bittermen, and the part of Schubert in the Kronenberg ads!

After Diana's critical acclaim as Jocasta in *Oedipus Tyrannus*, all that came her way were bit parts in *Keep It Up Downstairs*, *The Adventures of a Taxi Driver* and *The Adventures of a Private Eye*. To make ends meet, maintain a spacious mansion, pay Jason's school fees, and keep the tax man happy, Diana had to look for something else. She thought it was too early for an autobiography, so instead she would recall anecdotes from her life.

Having turned Jason's old nursery into a study, she took just two months to write *For Adults Only*. To help jog her memory and remind her of all her escapades and the famous people with whom she had come into contact, Diana completely covered all the walls in the room with photographs: herself with Jack Benny, Bob Hope, Doris Day, Ginger Rogers and Liberace – in fact, Diana Dors with almost every well-known name in the world of show business, plus stills from her many films, scenes from stage shows, and pin-up pictures. Each and every one had a story to tell from the thirty years of her life she had spent in the world of entertainment.

With the book at the publishers, Diana was able to accept a part on television playing Mrs Bott, Violet Elizabeth's mother, in 'Just William'. Bonnie Langford was the lisping Violet Elizabeth, and Jason, too, made his screen debut as one of the boys in William's gang. In January 1978 she went on a promotional tour for *For Adults Only*. Turning super-saleswoman she had no difficulty in persuading shops to order 100,000 copies.

It was due for general release on Valentine's Day. This was a day she and Alan always spent together, so she took a break from the whirlwind promotional tour. Diana awoke in Orchard Manor to be presented with a large red satin heart by Alan. With it was Robin Day's book, *Time for Lovers*, on the ecstasy and the disillusions of love. She handed him a poem she had written not many days before in an hotel room at St. Annes-on-Sea. It became Alan's most treasured possession.

What is A Lake?

'A Lake is a child-man who can never find the right clothes to wear at the right time, likes you to bathe and dry him, wash his hair and spoil him endlessly.

'He is a wonderful mixture of different things at different times, a man of many moods, loaded with personality, talent and sex appeal, shy and quiet *sometimes*, wild, uninhibited and defiant *most* times.

'A Lake can learn a whole play without study by merely using his photographic memory – yet can never remember people's names, or the places he is supposed to be at or how to get there.

'A Lake will quote Dylan Thomas at random, read Shakespeare aloud half-way through the night, drink too much, shout too much, and more than likely have a punch-up with anyone who challenges him, but give him a comic book and a bottle of pop in bed, and you'll never hear another sound all evening.

'He is super-sensitive, domineering, amusing, generous, egotistic, intelligent, sadistic, sweet and understanding. An exhibitionist with black curls which never go where they have been combed to go, dark sad eyes, and a smile which will charm the birds from the trees! One minute a reincarnated pirate complete with gold earring, flicking his sabre, another minute a little boy lost, desperate for love and affection.

'A Lake will aggravate, irritate and annoy you, fascinate, captivate and dominate you, worry you, protect you and comfort you, but *never* bore you. He is jealous, overpowering and larger than life, but he has the insecurity of a ten-year-old!

'A Lake can never sleep! Will keep you awake all night, for he is afraid of the dark and in the morning when he has deliberately woken you from a rest you *may* have been lucky enough to get, he will go off to sleep himself, leaving you to sit staring into space wondering what to do next.

'His mind is a fabulous structure of experiences and many pieces of knowledge, once learned and never forgotten. If he loves you then you are indeed favoured, but if he hates you, he will never let you forget why, and neither will he!

'He is quick tempered, quick witted, and quick to know if he has hurt you, but it takes him half an hour to put his clothes on in the mornings, and he can only concentrate on *one* thing at a time, so if he is watching television and you ask a question, don't expect an answer.

'Invite him to a cocktail party, and you will get a refusal, but he will spend all day and night at the local drinking beer and playing darts.

'A Lake will sing, dance, play the drums, mouth organ and spoons, mimic brilliantly, and act anyone off the stage, he will also shoot, fence and play cards at any time. He is passionate, unselfish and a *very* consistent lover, and if you can keep up with him you are quite a person. I try, and often fail, but in spite of this for some strange and mysterious reason, known only to him, he loves me.

'What is A Lake?

'He is above everything the man I worship, and love.'

These are words of love addressed to a man who was obviously very difficult to live with. Alan was often banished from the marital bed, and each time Diana found him curled up like a ball outside her door in the morning. Whatever state he was in, though, he always remained faithful to his wife and never caused her a moment's jealousy. When he went out for a game of darts and did not come back, he preferred open ditches for the night to the soft warm clutches of local girls.

Diana spent much of February and March marketing her book. One day when she arrived home, Alan had news for her. He had been offered a part in a film. When he told his wife that the production was called *Playbirds* and was a sex comedy in which he appeared with blue movie queen Mary Millington, Diana was not at all keen. But she knew too that in show business, if it was work, no matter what, you had little choice but to take it. Above all, this was a chance for Alan to try to show he could last the course without becoming maudlin on the set. His hopes were that passing this test would bring more work.

Boosted by the news of good sales for *For Adults Only*, the budding authoress got down to work on a sequel. This was called *Behind Closed Dors*. The format was the same, but her publishers asked for something a little more risqué than last time!

Now the writing bug had really gripped Diana, and having for the moment exhausted her reminiscences she began mapping out an epic novel.

Royalties were already accruing from *For Adults Only*, but not yet enough to appease the tax man. So, much against her own wishes, and putting aside her 'epic', it was back to the old routine again – cabaret.

One of the bugbears of Diana's life had been the continual encroachments of the tax man into her affairs. Hardly a week went by without some sort of missive being sent in the post marked 'Inland Revenue'. When work was meagre, she was once again threatened by the spectre of bankruptcy, and the worry of it affected little Jason too. Even at his tender age, he could sometimes understand his parents' breakfast conversations.

One day, when Diana was driving him to the set of 'Just William' he suddenly let out a big yell as they passed the Houses of Parliament.

"Quick, mummy, get down!"

Just able to avoid a collision, Diana shouted:

"What for? What's the matter?"

Pointing to the Houses of Parliament, Jason said:

"So that the tax man does not see you driving past in a Rolls Royce!"

In the New Year, Diana decided she would go to America once more. A few weeks earlier she had heard that Mark and his girlfriend had split up. Her eldest son was very upset. She phoned several times to do a mother's job consoling him, but it was hard going. Although able to control her emotions while talking to Mark, she shed many tears once she had replaced the receiver.

"If you're going to cry every time one of your sons has a broken love affair," said Alan, "I'd better take out shares in Kleenex."

Arriving in the States Diana had the chance to see the state of affairs for herself, and as it was three years since Alan had seen either Mark or Gary, he decided to go with her. Mark met them at the airport as he had the previous time. He was in much better form.

"I think I'm in love again." He greeted them with a big smile. The object of his love this time was Kathy, who worked alongside him on the set of *Family Feud*.

Gary, who was holidaying in Hawaii, returned a week later and the whole family began to pick up the threads of a very slender tightrope of affection.

Gary, like Mark, had decided on a career in show business. He impressed the visitors from England with his musical ability. He played piano, sang his own compositions and did impressions. Diana could not help but be reminded of a young Dickie, who in those early days had been so amusing, talented, and so very ambitious!

It was to further his career and to gain experience that Gary asked his mother as the time neared for their departure whether he could come back to England with them. There was no hesitation in Diana's reply! Dickie had no objection, so plans were hurriedly made and Gary returned with the Lakes in mid-January.

They had only been back in England just two weeks when Mark phoned to say he was marrying Kathy on March 4 1979.

This period with Gary was very much like the one she had spent with Jason during her fourth pregnancy.

"I can't get over it," said Gary, "for the first time in my life I've got someone I can really talk to, and sit down and discuss anything I want."

He told his mother that although Dickie had always been more than generous to Mark and himself, he was unable to communicate with them. This came as no surprise to Diana. Dickie had been no different with her. All the usual conflicts and confrontations between father and son Dickie found hard to understand.

Gary recalled:

"For years I never really understood my mother's part in my life. My father never encouraged my brother Mark or me to write or phone or think about her. He kinda made out she was an evil woman. I just assumed, because I was anxious to see my father's point of view, that she didn't want us. But that wasn't true. Having heard her side of things, I'm not at all surprised at the way things worked out."

There were a lot of other things Gary was to learn about his mother. For one thing, he had no idea that she was famous. He had never ever seen a film, a show or even a TV appearance. And when he was teased about how she was Britain's number one sex-symbol, he just laughed, "That doesn't matter to me. I love my mom and I'm proud she's my mother."

Diana had waited so long to hear this statement from son number two, and it meant the world to her.

16

THE FINAL CHANCE

Playbirds was released in the autumn of 1978. Its immediate success at the box office meant that Alan was signed up with co-star Mary Millington for a sequel called *The David Galaxy Affair*.

Diana was thrilled at the prospect of more months of work for her husband, and in case she still harboured fears of Alan's being tempted by scantily dressed females, she was offered a part as well!

But her main work in early 1979 was her latest book, *Behind Closed Doors*. This time the promotional tour was far more extensive than on the last book, even obliging her to go as far as Australia.

Naturally the visit to the Antipodes brought back memories of Darryl Stewart, and Diana found out that her one-time lover was still performing his act, and was still married to the woman he had forsaken all those years previously for Britain's number one bombshell.

Apart from being a best-selling authoress, Diana had only one remaining ambition. In her time she had been a guest on innumerable chat shows, ranging from John Freeman's to the one hosted by her friend Russell Harty. Now she wanted desperately to host her very own show. Garrulous at the best of times, there was no chance of Diana ever drying up in front of the cameras! When she heard that Southern Television were doing a series of pilot programmes for chat shows, she offered her services. The competition was severe. In contention were Anna Raeburn, former labour MP Helen Hayman, and Sue Slipman, the first woman president of the National Union of Students. There was also the local weatherman Trevor Baker, whose folksy fireside manner had made him very much loved. Diana did her pilot, interviewing Mary Whitehouse and Judy Carne.

She returned to Orchard Manor with the firm intention of continuing with her novel as the writing bug strengthened its grip. But Diana was soon to find herself right out of her depth, and it did not take too much persuasion from her publishers to get her to write her autobiography instead. After the flippancy of two collections of memoirs, she was prepared this time to write something more serious and to give her many fans an insight into the troubles and traumas behind the public image. Diana spent the early part of the summer of 1979 writing her life story.

She could not have been more content. Alan followed up *The David Galaxy Affair* with a supporting role in the film *Yesterday's Hero* with Ian McShane, with whom he had made *Sky West and Crooked*. He did a BBC television play called 'Destiny', and August found him telephoning daily from Northumberland, where he was working on another television series 'Blake's Seven'.

Diana's finances were boosted by the excellent sales of *Behind Closed Doors*, which in its first months outsold her previous book. Gary had settled well in England and each day saw him setting out in the black Ford Granada his mother had bought him to go to Guildford, where he attended the Guildford School of Music. Jason came home from boarding school, as Diana would be on hand herself to protect him should her husband go on a 'bender'.

Alan had proved that despite his craving he could still put in a 'performance'. As he would say:

"I may be an alcoholic but I'm an actor first."

If necessary he could go without a drink in the mornings, or all day for that matter, if he was working. He never lost a day on the set through drinking, but his performances were not up to the standards his wife believed him to be capable of.

In December 1979, Diana made headlines again. The Inland Revenue took out a High Court writ against her for £12,000 owed in income tax, surtax and interest from 1972. Although she put in a disclaimer to the press, saying that she knew nothing about it, Diana immediately put all her other activities aside, and engaged herself once more on a cabaret season in the run-up to Christmas.

This legacy from her frivolous days was a constant source of anguish to the Lake household, especially with a manuscript to be finished by the end of March. It even overshadowed the news that she had won the contract to host the chat shows. There were to be six half-hour chat shows called 'Open Dors' beginning in January 1980. Topics ranged from pornography – which she discussed with Lord Longford, the anti-porn campaigner, and Paul Raymond, of 'Raymond's Revue Bar' – to religion, debated by Bishop George Reindorp, retired Bishop of Salisbury, and Wolf Mankovitz, an avowed atheist. Diana even had the confidence to try out some of her newly-formed Catholic beliefs on the unsuspecting Bishop Reindorp.

Alan's mother, Millicent Lake, died of cancer on January 25 1980. It was a sad time for them all, but it affected Alan more markedly than it did the others in the family. Always very close to his mother, he sought to drown the sadness and pain in the only way he knew. Now followed weeks in which Alan forgot what it was like to be sober. When Diana and her sons returned from their hotel refuge one weekend in March, they found Alan lying in a crumpled heap against the living room wall. Diana said:

"It's no good Lakey, you know . . . you've just got to go back to Northampton."

"Yes, I know that, Di." There were no arguments this time, no justifications. "I'll go."

On previous visits there, Alan, like all alcoholics, had difficulty in accepting that he was one. He was convinced he came into the category 'heavy drinker'. Now in group therapy sessions, he mixed with men and women who admitted to being dependent on drink. They were ordinary people like himself, and it made him face the truth for the first time. He had been unwilling to do so before, partly because he could see no alternative to the life style he was used to. His whole social world centred on pubs.

But when, as part of the treatment, he was taken to a public house, Alan found that he could have the self-same camaraderie without the stimulus of alcohol. He came to see how embarrassing his addiction was for Diana, Jason and Gary, as well as the misery it had caused them.

When his wife visited the clinic, she told Alan she could not take him back again.

"This time, Di," Alan protested, "I'm cured. I realise I'm an alcoholic, and I'll never touch a drop again. Just give me two weeks. See how it works. If it doesn't, I'll go away. One last chance – please."

Diana agreed.

The first thing Alan did on leaving Northampton was to try to lose his beer paunch and get back in trim. Parts were coming his way after many fallow years, and he wanted to make the most of them. His greatest desire now was to act as the man of the house, to be responsible, and to win back Diana's affection by first regaining his own self-esteem.

After 'Blake's Seven', he appeared in 'Dick Turpin' for ITV, and his wife was able to land a role in a special two-hour version of Dick Turpin's adventures. She took the part of a scrubber in charge of a gang of beauties in a hilarious wash-house scene, where they all attempted to seduce Dick Turpin, played by Richard O'Sullivan.

For most actors and actresses, television was now their bread and butter. Very few films were being made. J. Arthur Rank had been going through a lean time with film production. Few were surprised when this side of their enterprise was abruptly closed in June 1980. For Diana, who had been created by Rank, it was a great blow:

"It's like someone dying. The British film industry was something of a joke until this flour millionaire came along and created a great new industry. They controlled Denham, Pinewood and what are now the BBC television studios at Lime Grove.

"Many big stars of the films have died or settled in America or on the Continent, but there's still a wealth of talent here that could make wonderful films. But people these days seem only to want to watch porn films, sex and violence – and that's where the money is. It's terribly sad."

Alan's list of TV appearances for '80/'81 is long. Parts came up in 'The Sweeney', 'Crown Court', 'Angels', 'Juliet Bravo', 'The Black Stuff', 'Rumpole's Return' and a major part in the play *The Olympian Way*. When the latter had finished, it was back to his first love, the theatre. This was another Edgar Wallace, *On the Spot*, which was performed at the Churchill Theatre, Bromley. He played the lead as Tony Pirelli.

To Alan, there was nothing in an actor's life that could measure up to the theatre. He loved the smell of greasepaint, peeping through an opening in the curtains and sizing up the audience, waiting in the wings, and then playing up and relating to the people in the auditorium. The atmosphere of the theatre got the best out of him.

Writing her autobiography took a lot of Diana's time and, like her husband, she too was busy in television. She also appeared in plays, made many guest star appearances on comedy shows, and was adept at panel games. But it was another series of Chat Shows that pleased her most. Southern Television gave her another series of 'half hours', this time called 'The Diana Dors Show'. It was day-time viewing, aimed at working housewives. As well as interesting chat, it was Diana's intention to bring a little glamour to the screen again. So when the programmes began in the winter, she went to the set dolled up to the nines, in 'designed-for-her' dresses and with her neck, arms and fingers covered in costly jewellery.

1980, by and large, was an 'at home' year for Mr and Mrs Lake, and, because of Alan's self-discipline, the happiest they had ever had. It was a chance to be a real family. Working on her book in the early morning gave Diana a lot of free time during the day. In the summer months there were lazy, carefree afternoons in the garden. Diana and Alan spent most of their time together, whether in the house or sunbathing side by side holding hands, and always talking to one another. Alan could not believe life could be so happy.

"At first when people stop drinking they think, 'Well, that's the end of all the fun because I can't stand in a bar any more with a drink in my hand'. And then you find that you have much more fun when you don't drink. At least *I* have; and I've made more real friends. But I'm more content just to be with Diana. I want nothing more than that.

"Mind you, it wasn't easy at first to adjust. But then when you begin to realise how good it is just to feel healthy all the time, there's no better feeling in the world.

"I think one of the biggest changes in my life is that I'm not afraid like I used to be. I don't wake up screaming at nights any more. I used to be afraid of the simplest things, like meeting new people. There was always this anxiety within . . . I just couldn't stop still, had to be doing something . . . and that was normally drinking. Now the simplest things appeal more."

A favourite family activity was picnics. Irrespective of the weather, Diana had everyone up, dressed and carrying sandwiches and flasks. The outings were always recorded in the family photograph album, to be relived again on winter evenings.

In 1981 a Lodge was erected near to the gates of Orchard Manor. It was ideal for Jason and Gary, and for Diana too, who hated having to curb the boys' enthusiasm in the house when she was trying to write and Alan to read his lines. It meant they could make as much noise as they liked, playing the guitar, singing and even composing songs.

After Alan's cure, Orchard Manor came back to life, and people began visiting again. Diana was always in her element entertaining. What gave her the greatest pleasure, as it had always done, was to have guests for dinner, so that she could prove her prowess as a cook and raconteur. She also enjoyed showing off their dining room. Unlike the rest of the house, which was very much Diana, and for the most, pink, this room was strictly Alan: muted colours, with beautiful antique furniture and tasteful oil paintings illuminated by hidden strip lighting. Heavy silver candelabra and place settings gleamed on the long, polished table, with the dumb-waiter ready to present delicate coffee cups at the end of the meal.

In 1981 work began on the swimming pool. This had been Alan's idea, as it was the only thing missing from their Hollywood-style home, and he knew how much Diana loved to swim. It would be the best money could buy.

In October 1981 *Dors by Diana*, her autobiography, was published. She was also able to introduce herself to a whole new world of fans by appearing on a video with pop star Adam Ant, who asked her to dress up and play the part of a Fairy Godmother.

The big event, though, that Christmas, was the opening of their new swimming pool. And to make sure it got an appropriate christening, Russell Harty came down with cameras and lights to do a programme about it.

Viewers must have gasped at the extravagance. Large, ornate gold-plated doors led from their spacious cream and pink lounge to the pool. Sliding the door open one might be forgiven for thinking one had stepped back to Greco-Roman times. The water was lit from below with multicoloured lighting, and surrounded, by marble columns, with a large stained glass mural at the far end. A happy, smiling Alan stepped aside and let his wife, in a one-piece swimsuit tailored to suit her ample proportions, be first into the water. Her fingers covered in sparkling jewels, rested lightly on the heads of two life-size statues of black panthers, sitting on their haunches at the top of the steps. Then, amid cheers from their assembled guests, she descended slowly until the water covered her ribs.

It was certainly a different setting for the Russell Harty show, and ideal for the party which came afterwards. Alan, now hooked on Perrier water, made an able pot-man in charge of a bar which his wife did not fear to keep well stocked.

The night was a triumph for Alan. The swimming pool was something that he himself had always wanted to buy his wife. Its building was the climax of a marvellous two years together. He had stuck to his resolution never to drink again, and they had spent more time together than at any other point in their married lives.

"Like twin oaks," Diana said, "we have intertwined and taken root."

17

THE INNER JOURNEY

Diana Dors once said, "If I go through twelve months without something happening to me, then it is a miracle."

In fact, that miracle lasted twenty-four months, until one fateful day in June 1982. During the morning Diana experienced severe stomach pains. Thinking they would go away, she continued working in the kitchen on preparations for the evening meal. By afternoon the pains had worsened until, doubled up in agony, she was rushed to hospital in an ambulance.

"We thought it was a burst appendix," Alan said, "but when they operated they found that an ovarian cyst had ruptured. It took them three hours to mop up the area. Then they gave me the bad news. The cyst had been malignant. Diana had cancer."

It was thought better that Alan should first keep the news to himself. The strain was tremendous as he talked, laughed and joked with his wife.

"Inside, I was terrified because of my previous experience of loved ones dying from cancer."

It came as a great relief to him when Diana too was told. They held on to each other sobbing, like two frightened children.

"When they told me, it was a terrifying jolt. No, no, no, I said, you've got it wrong. It can't happen to me ... I'm not the cancer type.

"A specialist said I was a brave lady – I was not, I was scared stiff."

Although Diana came through her operation marvellously, the doctors advised her to have a good rest and not to take on any engagements for at least six weeks. Alan cancelled a trip to Jersey for the filming of 'Bergerac' to be with his wife. At first she made a tremendous fuss about it, but was glad in the end that he insisted on staying.

Diana had to check into Charing Cross hospital every week for two days and two nights to undergo chemotherapy. Alan, as he always did when she was ill or in hospital, never left his wife's side. A folding bed was provided so that he could always be near.

The chemotherapy consisted of a drip to feed toxic drugs into the system. Diana's reaction to this treatment was severe. She vomited as often as five times in any one hour. She did not complain, however, believing that it was making her better.

It was quite a reversal of roles for the two of them. He had been dependent on her; now suddenly he was the strong one.

A couple of weeks after the operation, Diana insisted on travelling with Alan to Stoke-on-Trent. Glyn, Ken and Vilma's son, was being married.

"She looked absolutely marvellous," said her sister-in-law. "You'd never have known. She looked the picture of health and in surprisingly good form, chatting away as if nothing had happened, and keeping everyone amused with her quick wit."

The star never lost her sense of humour. She had this wonderful ability to laugh or joke in situations that would make most people cry. When the doctors told her that complete hair loss was normal with the treatment she was undergoing, expressing surprise that she still had her beautiful mane, she said, "Well, I can only think it's the years of bleaching that's preserved it! I haven't seen its natural colour since I was a girl."

One of her first thoughts on learning of her disease was that this experience would help her better to understand readers' problems in her new role as a *Daily Star* columnist. She wrote in her column, 'Sincerely Yours':

'I get all sorts of letters, some relating to illnesses. In the past I've had to refer the writers to a doctor. Now, I'll be able to give some first-hand knowledge.

"While in hospital, I replied to fourteen letters, and one in particular took my attention. It concerned a lady who had had a breast removed and was feeling down in the dumps because she didn't think her husband fancied her any more.

"I think I was able to help her a great deal."

When the doctors told Diana that she had cancer but that it was not too late to be cured, she was grateful to God. As far as she was concerned, He had stepped into her life again to save her, just as He had done when she had meningitis.

"I was very content and happy as a Catholic for several years, then I became smug and self-satisfied. I was pleased with my life and I didn't really need God's help any more. I thought He was far too busy coping with everyone else in the world. I just sort of shut Him out of my life for three years, and I'm ashamed to admit it. And then suddenly I was struck down again. This time I had cancer. If it had not been for God, and I know it was He from the way it happened, it could have gone on and on and I would have been dead eventually. Once again, I have been saved and once again I started to pray."

Perhaps the main reason behind her religious tepidity had been the fact that her great friend and mentor, Fr Simon, had left the priesthood. Father Simon had seen them most weeks for nearly two years while he was instructing them, and it was he who had received them into the Catholic Church. He had become a very close friend indeed and a frequent visitor at Orchard Manor. Diana said of him:

"Father Simon is a great friend of ours, and also the best advertisement for Catholicism that I know, as his views and outlook on life are very modern and updated, and he does not hide behind his Franciscan habit in a world of fantasy, like many other priests do."

Father Simon's leaving of the active ministry not only caused her great disappointment, sadness and sorrow, but also a feeling of being let down personally. Diana felt this more than her husband, because her faith was 'simpler'. Bishop Westwood who was on the radio with Diana at this time would later have this to say of her:

"Diana's faith was very simple, very straightforward, what I would call a pew Roman Catholic faith. She accepted the sacraments and the worship of the Church and that was it. She went to Mass. She couldn't tell me exactly what transubstantiation was...but it didn't matter. She believed she received the body and blood of Christ in the sacrament. She was at home."

To a great extent, initially anyway, she had associated her faith with Fr Simon and not with the Church at large. This is why it rocked her own belief considerably when her friend left the priesthood. Alan, on the other hand, continued to remain devout in the way he had when he first claimed the Roman Catholic faith as his own. The actor still found time for prayer and meditation, whether it was at Orchard Manor or Virginia Water, where, in the magnificent wooded lakeland of the National Trust property, he was often inspired to commune with the Almighty.

As God came crashing back into Diana's life, so did her determination to make up for the time she had lost in the spiritual wilderness.

"Now that I've rediscovered my belief in God," she said, "I would like, without wanting to sound a religious freak, to dedicate the rest of my life to Him, and to show my appreciation to Him by doing things which I feel He would like me to do...spreading His word in some way, in my own silly little way perhaps, showing people that I'm still alive and kicking after meningitis and the dreadful things that have happened to me. I'm back in church now and I'm there because I'm happy to be.

Theodore Fontanari was delighted at the return of the 'prodigal'. Diana remembered:

"I shall never forget the joy of Father's face when he saw me back at church again. 'Well, Father,' I said, 'I'm back now and you can expect me to be coming for the rest of my life.'"

For many years, both Alan and Diana had played a prominent part in parish life. They sang in the choir and attended practices. The actor and his wife also took it in turn to read the lesson.

"I could never understand why," said Fr Fontanari, "but

Diana was always very nervous about standing up before the congregation doing the Readings. It's surprising really, for someone so used to performing before large audiences!"

Later the Lakes stopped singing in the choir so that they could give more attention to the service.

"Another thing I noticed about them," said the priest, "was that they were always early for Mass. They arrived a good twenty minutes before everyone else and just sat together quietly in the front row."

Diana's regular correspondence showed how many listeners had been inspired by her faith and wanted to know more about Christianity from her. She wrote to each and every one, sharing with them her own feelings and experiences. She told Fr Fontanari one day that, if she were a priest and had a greater knowledge of God, she could help people more, but he assured her that it is not always the learned treatises of cloister and college that get through to people. She had an even bigger advantage, he said, and that was the wisdom that comes from having lived life to the full.

As part of the new-found wish to help people that being 'born again' gave her, she continued with her visits to Broadmoor, the top security mental hospital, just fifteen miles from Sunningdale. Ever since she had visited Alan in prison, she had known first-hand about the problems both prisoners and their families face.

When Ronnie Kray, who once ruled the London underworld with his twin brother Reggie, was transferred from Parkhurst to Broadmoor in 1980, Mrs Violet Kray, knowing of Diana's visits to the hospital, wrote and asked her to keep a special eye on her son. This she did, and wrote regularly to Mrs Kray.

Although Diana had never met the Kray brothers, they had been on the periphery of her life at Maidenhead, on the other side of the fence, as it were, attending rival parties at Dennis Hamilton's house next door. Perhaps now Ronnie was in a position to tell her who had thrown bricks through her windows!

Bishop Westwood said of her:

"Diana was a person who always seemed to be in God's presence and her real sense of the human touch made her a very powerful person indeed, without her even noticing it. She was a very real human being with an inner commitment."

Bishop Bill went on to explain that Diana could cope so well because in his opinion she had progressed in the inner journey:

"My wife is into Jung and she says we need to take the inner journey. Once past the age of forty we have to start looking at life and where we're going, and it is the time when many people begin to find the God who lives within them.

"I think in her own way Diana had begun the inner journey. How or when it happened, I don't know. Some people grow to it, some just come to it, while others have to fight terrible battles before they believe.

"Whatever it was, Diana had come to the time when the inner journey was one that she was starting to live."

Speaking on the 'Good Morning Sunday' programme, Diana gave the impression that the inner journey was something she grew to:

"Most of us have this fear of growing old and dying when we reach a certain age. Well, I'm now past fifty, and you start thinking when you get fifty-odd, often earlier, that life is more than half-way through, and I think this is the time when many people start thinking seriously about God and what will happen hereafter, which is a perfectly human thing to do.

"There are some perks in getting older. When you're young all you do is strive for your career . . . there are so many things to think about . . . that's why so many young people shut God out . . . not deliberately, but when you get older you know what you want, what you can tolerate, . . . yes, I'd love to be twenty again and be in the position I'm in now, knowing so much about life."

In her youth there had been only one ambition in her life and that was to be a film star, own a great mansion, with a cream telephone and a swimming pool. She had achieved this at a remarkably early age, and took it all as a matter of course:

"I made my mind up early that making pictures would be much better than watching them; being a film star was several notches better then dreaming about being one.

"Since I left school at thirteen I have been working for a certain standard of living. Once I'd got it, I saw no reason to give it all up. Luxury is comfortable, it's good for you, it's luxurious. And I liked it. Why shouldn't I?"

And yet when she arrived in Hollywood at the height of her fame and with a lucrative contract, she began wondering what all the striving had been about, and it left her with an empty, almost panicky feeling:

"One evening I sat alone in the pool-house among the orchids and the orange trees, gazing up at the big, floodlit white mansion. Coloured lights adorned exotic flowers and the sky-blue swimming pool, my dream since childhood, stretched before me illuminated in the dark. But I thought to myself, what happens now? This is all I ever wanted: I've achieved a life-long ambition. But where do I go from here?"

Success had blinded Diana to her own basic needs. The resolution that had for years proved strong enough to get her to the top suddenly evaporated as anger and the hunger for affection erupted from the depths of an outraged nature.

The failure of her emotional life and the prospect of never being able to have a genuine and deep love relationship filled her with despair. She had reached a point at which a lesser woman than Diana Dors would have gone the way of other stars and sex-symbols who no longer had box office appeal. Like them, she could so easily have turned to drink, drugs, taken an overdose or suffered a nervous breakdown.

But Diana was 'Britannia', as the public came to call her. With the bull-dog grit that was to win her so much admiration, she got to grips with her life. She looked for a new meaning to life, fresh values and different goals. Failure had proved the catalyst of change.

It was Alan who was immediately instrumental in leading Diana to God. Now it was up to God. Diana recalled again the first time she had entered the church of the Verona fathers:

"It was as if the hand of an angel swept past my face and stroked my cheek and something heavenly came over me and I received a great gift of peace."

It was an intense, beautiful moment, a rare occasion in life when one is suddenly brought to another and rarified level. Diana's conversion was a total gift of faith. It came unwarranted, unsought for and, so far as she was concerned, totally without merit or reason.

18

'A TOTALLY EXCLUSIVE ACTRESS'

In October 1982 Diana received the accolade of a second appearance on 'This is Your Life'. There were tributes from, among others, Bob Hope, Liberace and Richard O'Sullivan. Old friend Lionel Jeffries called her a "totally exclusive and brilliant actress".

A recorded message from America from her son was also a great joy to Diana.

"Hi, Mom," Mark greeted her, "I hope you're having a great night, and I hope you're recording it all for when you come out to California again."

Gary broke in, "It's three months since I saw you and Alan and Jason. I really miss you all and love you all. When I talked to you last it was great to hear you were back to your old self again. When you were taken ill you really gave us such a big scare. I've been thinking of all the things I kept meaning to put in all those letters I kept meaning to write!"

Diana smiled at that, but then her mouth opened wide, and she burst into tears when at the end of the show her two boys and Mark's wife Kathy walked onto the stage. It had been four years since she had seen Mark, and she was more than a little annoyed with him and with Kathy, because until her cancer operation they had not bothered to write or telephone. Diana was, of course, glad to find out that Mark was doing well with his rock band 'Midnight Eyes', and that Dickie's show 'Family Feud' was still top of the ratings, but the few days at Orchard Manor were not as cordial or indeed as 'easy' as she would have liked. Diana had to remind herself that Mark was a grown man, with his own life to lead.

In March 1983, TVam asked her to shed weight in public: fifty-two pounds to match fifty-two years of her life. It was another step by TVam's 'Good Morning Britain' to try to do something about their ailing viewing figures, following the demise of the 'Famous Five' presenters. Greg Dyke, editor-in-chief, knew Diana was one of the most popular figures on TV, because of her regular appearances on chat shows and panel games, and thought she would be ideal to feature in their new fun and competition package.

Diana had always wanted to appear regularly on TV, but the thought of going on a diet in public did not immediately appeal. There was one enormous drawback: would she be able to do it? Diana never could resist a sweet-trolley, and she and Alan loved nothing better than a curry at their local Indian restaurant!

Alan and Diana talked the offer over. If she were to succeed in her diet, then she would need the help and co-operation of her husband. He agreed, and she accepted. The star had also the support of twelve people who would join her on the slim-in.

The X-cel slimming programme was based on 1,000 calories a day, high in fibre and gelatine recipes. Miss Dors and her dozen weighed in on Friday June 28 at the plush Cannon's Sporting Club. Not being one for exercise, Diana hoped the surrounding aparatus was not part of the diet plan. It was not, so, a little more cheerfully, she stepped onto the scales.

Fearing she might not lose weight, Diana began to diet as soon as she agreed to go on the programme. Moreover, at the weigh-in she wore a kaftan, into the hem of which she had dropped some small lead weights to equal the pounds she had lost. Her plan was that if she fell by the wayside and did not lose anything when she began the X-cel diet, then she would gradually remove the lead weights!

But Diana did lose weight – she did not want to let her public down. Flaunting a figure whose pounds of fat had long ago buried a priceless one did not bother her one iota. She went on to demonstrate just how extremely glamorous one can look at fifty plus, even if one happens to weigh over 15 stones!

It was a shapelier Diana who, towards the end of August of

the same year, went back to her home town. Jim Masters, who had known Diana as a child, had been elected Mayor of Swindon for the year 1983/84. It was his suggestion that Diana, whom he had once called 'a snotty-nosed little girl', should return for the the opening of Vickers Airfield at South Marston.

"She looked terrific," said Jim, "much slimmer than when we saw her when she judged the 'Cook of the Year' competition in March. She looked lovely in her pink and white dress. She could still make the blokes' heads turn, and by gosh, couldn't she handle them all! But then, she always could, even as a tot.

"During the official reception after the opening, we all tried to make her eat, but she was having none of it. She just stuck to her guns. I expect anyone would when you have to appear before an audience like she had to every Friday morning!"

The Swindon annual Trade Fair was also being held on the airfield at the same time as the opening, and Diana did a walk-about.

Many stall-holders were disappointed that she did not get to them. The reason for this was that she had spent most of her time at the Cancer Research Stall.

Afterwards the Mayor took her on a tour of the old haunts they had known as children. Not much had changed in the old town of Swindon. The family home in pleasant Marlborough Road was there, but the private school she attended had been knocked down by redevelopers. Not that that broke Diana's heart!

During the drive around, Jim Masters told his guest for the day about a major operation he had recently undergone.

"This interested her a lot, poor dear. She kept asking me for details just as if she was comparing my operation with hers. Though she didn't say anything about herself, the impression I got was that she had an inkling that something was still wrong with her.

"And it was interesting, too, that when I told her that the old Manager's House in Railway Village had been turned into a Hospice for terminally ill people, she asked me to take her there."

The Hospice grew from an idea of a local man whose wife had died of cancer. He formed a committee and then got a sponsorship. From there on it grew and terminally ill patients were able to stay for a week or even two, to give both themselves and those who looked after them a break. Diana spent quite a while in the house talking to those in residence, and she was especially delighted when she spotted a large picture of herself on the wall.

The tour ended up in the New Town of Swindon, where the Mayoral limousine stopped beside a new precinct, the Brunel Shopping Arcade. Jim Masters had something to show Miss Dors. On a wall of the building was a giant mural of people who had won renown for Swindon. Dwarfing everyone else was the world famous engineer, Brunel, who brought the Great Western Railway works to Swindon; alongside him, just to prove that at least a little oil had been poured over troubled waters, there was a large head and shoulders portrait of Diana Dors.

19

DORS HAS DONE IT

Having first weighed in at 15 st 4 lb Diana was 14 st 5 lb on September 2 1983. She had lost the two pounds a week she was set out to do. She was on course, and TVam were delighted with her. What viewers did not see behind the smiling exterior of Miss Dors was her worry about another cancer operation next day.

The doctors had told her that she needed major surgery. 'A life-saving operation', was the way they had put it. She had kept this knowledge from Alan, fearing it would jeopardise the plum role he had just landed in the television series 'Hart to Hart'. Alan had flown off to Greece with the parting words, "Now look, darling, if you need me pick up the phone, I'm only a whisper away."

Before leaving for hospital, Diana phoned him. Thinking it was the usual daily call, the actor picked up the telephone cheerfully in the little taverna in which he was staying.

"Darling, I'm going into hospital for an operation, but don't worry, I'll be fine. And don't come rushing back." Diana repeated, "I'll be fine."

Immediately Alan's mind went back to 1982, when she was operated on to remove a cyst.

"I knew I had to get back. All flights to London were fully booked, but I was so desperate I even asked the American Air Force to drop me by parachute over Salisbury Plain."

Finally, he reached Amsterdam aboard a private jet and then managed to get a flight to London, arriving two hours before the operation was to begin.

"I was so upset, I couldn't believe God could do this to her again. She got very tough with me and said it had nothing to do with God. It was more to do with human frailty. She said, 'We must ask God for help. That's the way we'll beat this.' She never said, 'Why me?'. Because that would have meant somebody else suffering instead. And she wasn't like that."

When the operation was over, the doctors broke the news to Alan. Malignant cells had spread to the star's stomach. The cancer was back.

Once again, Alan was forced to keep this heartbreaking news to himself. The very next day, his wife, welcoming the cameras into her private room at the hospital, and buoyant with optimism, told viewers:

"They operated successfully. Took away the nasty bit and found absolutely nothing else. So, thanks be to God, I'm clear."

Alan had to return to Athens, where Robert Wagner and Stephanie Powers, the stars of 'Hart to Hart', anxiously quizzed him.

"She's just fine," he told them, with a lump in his throat.

Wagner had known Diana for many years. They had also appeared together on TVam a short while earlier.

"Cancer is a frightening disease," said Miss Powers. "It's great to hear of someone with grit fighting back like Diana is."

"I'd have been worried about leaving her," said Alan, "if she wasn't such a fighter."

Alan returned from Greece on September 7 to a wife who desperately needed his support and comfort. Three days later, she left hospital. The doctors wanted her to stay longer, but Diana had promised Jason that she would be home for his fourteenth birthday. There was a surprise for her when she reached Orchard Manor. Tied on the front gate was a huge white ribbon with the words:

"Welcome Home Mum."

Among the piles of 'Get Well' cards that greeted her on her return from hospital had been many from those who watched TVam. This prompted the show's producers to send Nick Owen to see Diana at Orchard Manor on October 7.

Seated in a leopard-skin chair beside the swimming pool in

a soft blue kaftan, Diana admitted, in answer to Nick's question, "Are you scared of cancer?":

"Yes, Nick, of course I'm scared. I don't want it to keep coming back, but then I shall fight it all the way; it's chosen the wrong person in choosing me. But then you see, you must never let this thing get you down because it's cancer.

"My faith in God has helped me through all this. You know, I've had an awful lot of books sent to me by well-wishers about *Mind Over Cancer, Diet Over Cancer,* and all sorts of theories about what one should or should not do. Basically, yes, I'm sure they're fine and I'm thankful to the doctors and the medical technology we have today – they're wonderful people and we're living in a great age where we can fight this sort of thing – but we can only do it if we're sensible ourselves. Basically, Nick, if you really want the answer, I'm scared, of course, but I know God is protecting me, and I don't know why He is saving me, but He's done it three times now and I just know there is no way in which He will allow me to have cancer again."

A week later Diana was back in the TVam studios, looking as stunning as ever. With just a fortnight to go before the final weigh-in, viewers were interested to see how the star's recent traumas would affect her weight loss. They need not have concerned themselves, for Diana weighed in at 11 st 10 lb, just four pounds off her target weight.

On the day of her final weigh-in, October 21, she stepped onto the scales at 11 st 5 lb. She had achieved her goal with a pound to spare, and therefore could celebrate her birthday by eating all the 'goodies' she wanted!

"Di hated the diet," said her sister-in-law. "She was very unhappy doing it. You see, she loved her food, she loved cooking. When they came to us, she used to say when I cleared the table, 'Don't put the food away Vil, leave it on the sideboard so I can help myself'. She loved sausage rolls and things."

When Diana agreed to do the 'Slim-in', it had been her hope that it would eventually lead to more work as an interviewer.

It did not, but it *did* lead to a spot as an Agony Aunt on TVam, to be called 'Open Dors'. This was a natural follow up to her 'Slim-in'. While she was dieting she had invited letters from viewers with weight problems, but as it happened, they were far more interested in her fight against cancer than in her losing weight, and felt that she could help them in a way others could not.

"Try not to feel sorry for yourself," she would say. "I refuse to let my two illnesses get me down. There is an old saying, you know, 'If everybody's troubles were put into a bag in the middle of the street you'd all run for your own.'"

Viewers loved Diana's no-nonsense approach. She received a tremendous amount of letters in response to 'Open Dors'. This moved her greatly.

"I find it very heartwarming that people feel they can write to me and I am in some way helpful to them with their problems."

Most people with problems are almost inevitably ridden with sadness, regrets and terrible feelings of guilt about their past. Like everybody else, Diana had black areas in her life of which she was not very proud.

"I've been no shrinking violet," she said.

Hamilton had, of course, exercised a tremendous influence on her behaviour. In their selfish go-getting days they cheated shop-keepers and landlords, making moonlight flits. They did not care for the feelings of those they hurt in their mad stampede to the top. At the parties she gave at Orchard Manor, drugs were always freely available. In fact, cannabis was grown in the garden.

When Nick Owen came to Orchard Manor after her second cancer operation she was open and frank:

"I've lived a wonderful life, but I have also been in my day a wicked so and so, I have. But I don't think that because I've got cancer, it is the wrath of God for things I've done in my youth."

Whatever Diana had done, she had reached the stage where she could live with her past. Bishop Westwood, not unaware of Miss Dors' reputation, was struck by the way she coped with her past:

"She was very easy about it. Now, there are lots of religious people who come to the faith late in life who find it difficult to accept their past. I believe that God gives us our past as well as our present and it is a denial of God not to accept your past, although difficult at times. She seemed to me to be a person who was easy with herself. I thought that was a great Christian gift."

It was this gift that Diana tried to impart to viewers who wrote to her about guilt for past misdemeanours. To one writer who had undergone an abortion, and whose continual crying and deep depression upset her husband and family, Diana showed a marked sympathy. She leaned forward in her chair and stared straight at the camera, as if talking to the lady personally:

"I have no solution for the terrible guilt and misery which I know you are going through. Only time and God's forgiveness can heal you.

"I don't know if you are a religious person at heart. I pray you are, because that is the only way. You have to come to terms with God to find total peace and happiness. Nobody on earth can give it to you. You've had your dance with the devil. You can see the misery it brings. Now is the time to blossom in God's love."

The letters Diana answered on television were just the tip of the iceberg. She often entered into correspondence where she thought it necessary. To receive a letter from Diana Dors was always a tonic.

Of the letters she received, the star had her own favourite:

"When I'm feeling really low, I close my eyes and imagine that I hear my doorbell ring. I go to the door, open it and find you standing there wearing one of your lovely pink dresses and all your jewels and I feel better immediately."

In the same week that she started 'Open Dors' in October 1983, she began her first column in the *News of the World*: 'Diana Dors... Straight from the Heart'. In it she wrote:

"Someone once said that only a fool celebrates getting a year older, and maybe they are right. But this year, one week into being 52, I really have reason to toast myself in champagne. Why?

Because yet again Dors has done it. And what have I done? Survived!

Having finished 'Hart to Hart', Alan was not keen to accept work. He wanted to stay with his wife. Whether, in fact, he would have been fit to work was another matter. Whereas Diana was able, with her accustomed bravado, to face the world head-on when the cancer re-occurred, Alan was not. He was devastated, and within weeks turned from a man full of confidence and in command of life, to a nervous wreck.

"It was a terribly sad time," Fr Fontanari recalls. "Diana, of course, was far from well, and Oh, poor Alan! I had this five-page letter from him. It was awful. He said I had neglected him, turned away from him altogether, didn't care any more, and neither did the Church. I was shocked and phoned the house directly. Diana said it was no good coming over, because he was in a bad state. I went anyway. Diana let me in: 'He's upstairs, but it's no good going up. Alan's banging his head against the wall. I can't do anything for him.'

"I knew what it was. When Diana was ill again, he could not face the thought of losing her. The fear of losing her was just driving him crazy. He just went berserk. He was having no sleep."

Unable to relax, Alan went sleepless for days and nights on end. He was not still for one moment at a time and talked non-stop – to himself, if no one else was nearby. In an effort to dispel some of his excess energy, he often swam in the pool, particularly during the night when his wife was in bed. He also stayed in the jacuzzi for long periods, letting the gurgling warm water gently massage his aching limbs. But while it soothed his body, it did nothing to help his mind. When eventually, through utter exhaustion, sleep came, Alan did not wake up for two days. Then he was as hyped up as ever. At times Diana had little patience with him. Not being well herself, and with a very demanding work load, the strain told.

"Quite often she would snap at him and tell him to go to bed as if he were a naughty boy," said one of her friends.

Diana could not understand what was happening to Alan.

For one thing, she did not know that her husband knew the seriousness of her illness.

Most people have very little conception of the severe anxiety that accompanies mental disturbances. Even when Diana was unkind to Alan, it was she who received the sympathy of friends, not the husband. Had the actor been suffering some physical illness, sporting, for example, a broken limb, then people would have been more understanding.

When her husband's condition worsened and she realised it was more then just 'being depressed', Diana went to their general practitioner for help. The doctor formed the opinion straight away that Alan needed proper medical attention. The problem, though, was to persuade the actor to go back into hospital. In the end Diana prevailed and Alan went to the Cardinal Clinic at Oakley Green, not far from Windsor, which specialises in psychiatric disorders. It was then Diana understood that what she had found so 'trying' about her husband was in fact a severe disturbance brought about by the fear of losing her.

Father Fontanari was as ever anxious to do all he could to help.

"It was a very down time for them both," said the priest. "When Alan returned from hospital, I gave him a Bible with gold-leaf pages. I thought it might help him. It was then Diana asked me if it were possible for them to have Communion on Saturday instead of coming to Mass on Sunday. They couldn't face people, you see. Both of them were so very ill."

Alan and Diana guested on the 'Cilla Black Christmas Show', recorded in November. Though much better, Alan still looked nervy and jumpy. Once the couple had done their party piece, Alan seemed only to want to be close to his wife. He constantly put his lips to her cheek.

Throughout November, Alan began to improve. The fact that Diana had not only coped well with her commitments, but also improved in health, restored Alan's faith that, after all, she was an unsinkable dreadnought, and that those frequent trips to

Charing Cross hospital were at last paying dividends. Diana's improvement was the gauge of his own.

Diana, Alan and Jason spent the Christmas period happily together behind closed doors. They felt they had turned the corner at last. When Vilma and Ken came, as they usually did, to celebrate the New Year, they noticed a considerable improvement in both brother and sister-in-law. Vilma said:

"Diana always had the Christmas tree left up until we got there. Then we had to have a bottle of champagne. Alan always had one ready in the fridge, and a bottle of Perrier water for himself. We had to toast the New Year, because every New Year was going to be a better one, and we all really believed that 1984 was going to be the best. We really believed that.

"You see, Alan was so much better. He'd put back the weight he'd lost. He looked more himself, because in October, he was really dreadful. And as for Diana, well, she looked absolutely wonderful. Things seemed to be going right at last and we were all very happy."

With the new year of 1984 well and truly in, both husband and wife were busy working. While Diana wrote her columns, appeared on 'Open Dors', and dealt with mountains of correspondence, Alan was travelling up and down to London doing 'voice-overs' and acting in TV commercials again.

Both were absolutely sure that this time, the cancer was beaten.

20

THE PRICE SHE HAD TO PAY

It was a very cold February morning when Diana, now looking very slender in a pink track suit, talked to Nick Owen on TVam:

"Well, Nick, you won't be seeing me for a while. On Monday I start a film with Vanessa Redgrave called *Steaming*, which is taken from a play which was a great success on Broadway and the West End."

The film, directed by the renowned Joseph Losey, revolves around six women who meet once a week at the steam baths to discuss the men in their lives.

"Do you know," added its co-star, "I shall be up earlier than you, Nick, for the next couple of months!"

Diana kept fighting for her fans, but mainly for Alan. She worried how he would cope were she not around.

One crew member who was on the set at Pinewood said:

"Diana was absolutely sensational. She put everything she had into it. She was on the set at 6 am every day, and was never late – and she looked her best at all times. In fact, everyone kept complimenting her on how marvellous she looked.

"She used to joke then: 'When you're in your fifties, darling, you have to try harder.'"

It was during *Steaming* that the doctors changed her treatment and put her on a course of cancer-killing tablets. She placed great store in these.

Mrs Honor Webb, who looked after the Lake home, was of the opinion that her employer never thought the cancer was fatal.

"One day she showed me a swelling she had on the left side of her tummy, and then she gave it a friendly little pat, and said, 'Look Honor, the pills are working."

Self-deception was never a part of Diana's make up, so it is surprising that she seemed not to suspect that her disease would eventually kill her. Her faith that God would cure her was unshakeable. As for the usual tell-tale signs such as weakness and loss of weight, the star was quick to find a rational explanation. The debilitating twinges of pain she put down to the side-effects of her cancer-curing treatment. The consistent loss of weight and appetite was camouflaged by her 'Slim-in'. During the many months of stepping onto the weighing machine at TVam, Diana's eating habits had changed considerably, and even when she had shed four stone and the 'Slim-in' came to an end, she found it very hard to alter them. When her stomach began to reject certain types of food she thought it was because it had shrunk during her long regime. Besides, she enjoyed her new curvy figure and rather cherished the reminder of her starlet days. And she really did look extremely good. Mrs Webb says that Diana was so slim she just could not take her eyes off her:

"Mrs Lake was so beautiful and looked no more than sixteen years old with her flawless skin and hair tied back in bunches."

When Diana invited reporters to interview her, she went to a lot of trouble to prepare herself:

"After all the reporters had gone, she would give me a little wink and say, 'Honor, that's what people expect of Diana Dors! But I don't look upon myself as Diana Dors. I'm two people. I know who I am at home, but the rest of the time professionally, I'm pretending to be her. See, I just hate the way I look, loathe seeing myself, loathe the whole blonde image.

"I still hate dressing up because that means being Diana Dors, and that means work, and I never wear make-up unless I have to. That's why my skin's so good."'

She was still paying the price for her sex-symbol days. The luxury and the glamour were part and parcel of being a film star, and for the British public, Diana, more than anyone else, typified what a star must be like. The world of tinsel and stardust would never be allowed to leave her. She would always be expected to turn up for her engagements in either a Cadillac or a Rolls Royce, and to be driven everywhere by a chauffeur, to wear the most fantastic creations, and to keep that long, platinum blonde hair cascading copiously around her shoulders.

"If only I could get rid of this," she used to say at home, touching her hair, "I'd really love to get it cut off and stop bleaching it and let my own colour grow through. But I can't. People expect Diana Dors to look like this, so there's nothing I can do about it."

For the public, Diana always wore low-cut dresses. At home it was a different matter. She was modest to the point of being a prude. The kaftans she often wore around the house all had high necklines, and even in their own private pool where she swam daily, she always wore a one-piece costume.

It was Diana's boast that she never appeared naked in a film. She was glad to have been a starlet in the times she was one:

"If I was fourteen today and wanted a career as a film actress, it would be so hard to begin. They have to do all sorts of things to get into films. We have no film industry and many of the films are of a high pornographic level. Good films lose money, while pornographic romps make a fortune."

Diana disliked the present high level of nudity and protested openly about it on many occasions. She hated the lurid display of 'girlie' books in newsagents, and made headlines by taking local newsagents to task about it:

"The place for them is Soho, not Sunningdale, and not in view of children who come in to buy sweets."

Diana was genuinely upset by it all:

"In the old days things were left to the imagination. Sex was hardly mentioned. Titillation was the right word for it. Now, when I look back on my life I think how perfectly harmless it all was.

"Looking back I, too, think the world of entertainment was a nicer place. Duller, perhaps sillier in many ways, but it was something to make sex seem an exciting possibility without actually offending or harming anybody."

At home she was determined to be plain Mrs Lake, the name she rejoiced in. When not in kaftans she wore track suits. And it was in the latter, with hair tied back in bunches with ribbons, that she did her chores as wife and mother.

In Sunningdale the people treated her quite naturally:

"They're used to seeing me with no make-up, jeans, hair in a tangle. But one day for no reason at all I looked smart. 'Oh,' said one woman behind the counter, 'going somewhere nice?'

"It's a pity though as a celebrity you can't normally do the everyday things you would like to. People expect you to be on the stage all the time. I tried to disguise myself once, a dark wig, dark scarf and dark glasses and no make-up. I went with Alan to Windsor races. 'Hello, Miss Dors,' said someone immediately I got out of the car."

Diana was most relaxed at home with Alan and Jason; they were then 'The Three Musketeers', as she affectionately dubbed them. Her first cancer scare had only increased her love and affection for husband and son. She knew that sometimes in the past she had taken them for granted. Now, with the Sword of Damocles hanging over her head, she was much more patient and tolerant.

"So many things which used to get on my nerves make me smile now. When my husband leaves his clothes cluttering up the bedroom I don't get annoyed any more. That reminds me that I'm home and things are just the way they always were, thank goodness."

Diana's fervent prayer was that they would remain that way. She believed that as the doctors had only given her some tablets costing £1.40 to make her better, her condition certainly was not serious.

"Mind you, she remarked with a laugh, "they *do* look like horse pills!"

On the set of *Steaming* the star looked fit as well as beautiful.

"She had lost weight," Felicity Dean, one of her co-stars,

recalls, "and seemed in wonderful spirits. She didn't give any hint of how ill she was. She was professional as an actress and wouldn't inflict it on anyone. She would do what she had to do with a minimum of energy and then go off to her room or sit down. She never told anyone."

Sarah Miles, also a co-star, corroborates this:

"Diana was great fun to work with. She kept us in fits of laughter all the time, and no one knew what she was going through."

Diana was a dab hand at disguising her pain, especially where Alan and Jason were concerned.

"I remember," said Honor, "when she was at home and Mr Lake was out filming somewhere. Every time he phoned up she brightened straight away and put on the most soothing voice, reassuring him that everything was fine and that she felt quite alright.

"But she was in a lot of pain. I knew it because I saw it. There are mirrors everywhere at Orchard Manor, and when she was coming out of the downstairs cloakroom I could see her face. She didn't know I could see her, but the agony was written all over it. The minute she spotted me she put on her beautiful smile.

"I always loved going to work there. I got very excited about it. They were such lovely people to work for. She was a star, a real star, one of the greatest. And what I admired about her was her strength, and the wonderful way she always 'played the game'".

21

THE WORLD HAS LOST
A LEGEND

On Palm Sunday, April 15 1984, the Lakes went to Mass at the Sacred Heart Church. Diana was pale and drawn and Fr Fontanari noted that she had great difficulty walking:

"She had on a black fur coat. It was rather cold, and she sat with Alan in their usual place. Throughout the service she seemed to be very poorly. Her breathing was heavy and when she knelt down to pray she couldn't get up again and Alan had to help her. She looked as if she was going to faint. When they came to receive Communion, Alan almost had to carry her.

"Afterwards, outside, I took Diana's hand and asked if she was feeling better now she was outside. She said to me, 'Oh, yes, Father, I'll be alright. The fresh air is very nice.'"

During the following week Diana said:

"I am experiencing some new and rather nasty side-effects from the tablets now ... and they have taken my appetite away altogether. I can only manage a little fruit or yoghurt."

A few days later the crippling stomach pains came back again and she spent a week in bed. Alan tenderly looked after his wife. He bathed her, changed and fed her with a little Complan. But by now she was unable to keep anything down and vomited it straight back again.

During this week, and despite her condition, Diana planned a holiday that they would take as soon as she felt better. They decided on Spain.

By the weekend the pains she was experiencing were so violent that she was taken on a stretcher to the Princess Margaret hospital in Windsor.

Alan told Fr Fontanari:

"We are all pretty certain that the intestinal problem is

totally unrelated to the cancer. She is still winning her fight and has been responding well to the course of drugs she was put on."

On Sunday evening, April 29, the priest phoned his friend:

"Diana, we're praying for you. Mass was said for you today."

"Oh Father," Diana's husky voice was heard, "I'm sure God will help me. My priority is my faith in God, my second is my faith in doctors. Thank you for your prayers. Tell them I'll be fine. I'll be alright."

The following day, Monday 30, the operation to remove a blockage was performed and, although it went well, the doctors discovered that the cancer had spread throughout her body, even to the marrow of her bones.

Alan was at his wife's side as always, resting when he could on the folding bed the nurses had put there for him. In the morning the doctors broke the news to him.

"I saw Mr Lake through the camera and immediately opened the gates for him," said Mrs Webb. "He looked very tired and pale. I asked him if he was alright. 'Yes, I'm alright Honor. But it's Diana. I've got bad news for you. The doctors said she's perhaps only got two more weeks to live, although it could be up to three months.'

"I could see he was just speaking words. He couldn't accept it, you see. They had made so many plans for the future. To him she was so strong, unconquerable, indestructible. He couldn't believe it was happening. He acted quite normally, just as if the news had not sunk in."

Having told Jason that his mother was doing alright though still very ill, Alan went back to the hospital. Fr Fontanari was there. The afternoon had brought numerous 'Get Well' cards from friends and fans alike. The room was bright and airy and Diana looked as fresh and beautiful as the myriads of bouquets and baskets of flowers surrounding her.

"She was in good form," Fr Theo remembers. "Like always she did all the talking. She said to me, 'Oh, I could have done so much more for God as a Catholic actress. People would have listened to what I said. When I get better' – she said 'when', 'not if' – 'I will start a programme, Alan and myself on religion. God...and faith.'

"This had long been a cherished desire of Diana's.

"And all the time she talked Alan just sat there looking at her. He thought it was wonderful the way she went on talking about God. And he kept on saying all the time, 'Diana, I love you'.

"When I was with her, before he came, she kept talking about them both – that's Alan and Jason. God must have given that family something special because they stuck together for better for worse.

"Anyway, I thought she was making herself very tired with all that talking and I told her so. When I got up to go, she took me by the arm, though there was no strength in her grip, so I sat down again. She took my hand and said:

"'Yes, Father, I am tired, but I must tell you how I feel. Do you know, Father, on Easter Sunday I had so much pain, so much pain!' She gave a big sigh. 'Words kept ringing in my ears. Words of Jesus on the cross: 'I'm thirsty'. I do not know why, but I couldn't stop them. They kept ringing in my ear all the time. So I thought, Jesus suffered for me, and that helped a lot. But you know, I thought God had left me, but he hadn't.'"

When Fr Theo took his leave of Diana that Tuesday afternoon she was very cheerful. She told her husband that she was going to get better because she had too much to do to be ill. On Wednesday Jean Rook wrote in the *Daily Express*:

'Di, a nation is praying for you, pulling for you. You're our solid 'Golden Oldie', the very best of unbeatable British. You've shown more guts than they've taken away and we love you and are proud of you for what you've been for fifty-two glorious years. Our own. Bounce back, soon!'

And it looked for a short while as if she was going to bounce back. She talked a lot about the holiday in Marbella which they had planned just before her entry into hospital.

The next day, however, saw a change in her condition. The doctors told Alan that his wife's other organs were not functioning properly. She was deteriorating fast.

In the early hours of Friday morning Fr Fontanari was called to the hospital:

"It was a very dark morning. There wasn't a soul about as I motored through Windsor Great Park. At the hospital I rang the bell and was let quietly in. All was dark apart from a little blue light beside the bed.

"I saw Diana. She was covered with something and had a wet cloth over her head. She was very feverish. Alan said to her, 'Father's come, darling.'

"'Ah, Father. I've had a very bad night. I'm very tired.'

"I said to her, 'Hello, Diana, I've brought you Communion.'

"'Thank you, Father.'

"So I said, 'Let's pray together.'

"She said a few prayers and she made a beautiful sign of the cross. I anointed her and said a few prayers, but the 'Our Father' she said after me. Though she was very weak she was fully conscious. Once or twice she breathed really heavily, then she said, 'Jesus, I love you. Mary, Mother of Jesus, help me.'

"Then she made another sign of the cross, very weakly this time. It was her last sign as a Christian. It was very beautiful. Then her breathing became difficult... very heavy. 'She is bad,' I said to Alan. But she didn't look bad, and she understood every word. They say when somebody dies the last sense to go is hearing, so I said another short prayer, and I said, 'God bless, Diana... goodbye, I'll see you tomorrow.'"

When daylight came, Alan left the room for a short while. The nurses came to attend her. On his return he had the surprise of his life.

"She was propped up with pillows. Her blonde hair beautifully brushed out. She wasn't wearing the usual hospital garb but her own favourite shorty nightie in white cotton with green and red polka dots. My sister Vilma had given it to her and she loved it. She often used to wear it to wander round our lovely large garden.

"I could hardly believe my eyes. She looked no more than sixteen, and so beautiful. I knew the nurses had dressed her like this because the end was near.

"All I could think about was that I had the most beautiful wife in the world and I loved her more than words could ever say.

"They even put her gold necklace with the letters D-O-R-S round her neck again. She loved that necklace and only took it off for the operation. She was smiling.

"'They've put your necklace on upside down, darling,' I said, 'I'll put it on right for you.'

"Then I looked into her eyes and I knew she knew the truth. 'I love you,' I said, and I just kept on repeating it. She replied, 'Oh my darling, I love you. Yes, I love you. Oh, I feel so spoilt. Please thank everyone for their concern and their prayers.' Then she whispered, 'I love you and the boys. Look after them for me. I love you.

"I leaned down close to her face and said, 'Remember always, my darling, I'm only a whisper away at any time. I love you.'"

When she went into a coma Alan knew the end was very near but he could not stop himself from doing all he could to call her back. To his amazement she did open her eyes.

"Why did you call me back? Why?"

Alan was stunned. He wanted to say, 'because I love you', but the words would not come out.

"I was a bit upset with myself really, because she seemed to be half-way into another and more wonderful world and here I was pulling her back into this one. Then she went again, and this time I said nothing. I just sat holding her hand and staring at her.

She looked so young and absolutely at peace, and that's what gave me so much comfort when that last breath left her lips. The nurse beside me got up and went to get a doctor, but I knew it was the end before he came in and said 'I'm terribly sorry.' Nevertheless I couldn't stop myself from breaking down completely."

When Alan regained his composure the news had spread and the press were in the corridor downstairs asking for him.

"I didn't feel strong enough to see them, but I knew Diana belonged to everybody and not just to me. She went through some tough times in her life, but she always faced up to the world. She never ducked out and neither would I. So I told them all quite simply, 'I have lost my wife and soul mate. My son has lost a friend and mother, and the world has lost a legend!'"

Diana had always accepted suffering as part of being human, but gradually she came to see that it had an important part to play in the greater scheme of things. And that was her final message to her countless fans and admirers, particularly those who had shared their problems with her and had come to rely on her help. To Diana suffering was never meaningless or pointless. From the start she was able to see in her cancer the dark hand of God's caress. It had stopped her in her tracks when she was complacent, it deepened her sorrow for the way she had treated God, and it advanced a wonderful woman further along the road of perfection, finally preparing her in a way nothing else could, for the afterlife.

She said:

"I think these things are sent to try us here on earth and test us through this life to see how we come through, so that at the end of the day, we know whether we warrant eternal life or not."

22

"WE MUST BE GRATEFUL
THAT WE HAD SO MUCH"

The Requiem Mass and funeral service for Mrs Alan Lake took place exactly where she herself would have chosen, the Church of the Sacred Heart, Sunningdale. The service was conducted by her dear 'little' Italian priest, with Fr Dominic and Fr O'Sullivan, who had succeeded Fr Simon as Parish Priest of Englefield Green, assisting.

The legendary glamour girl of the silver screen had been placed in a golden oak coffin, clothed in her most sensational evening gown of gold lamé with a matching full length cape. Thick platinum blonde hair, combed gently over her shoulders, framed in a now tiny face. Around her neck the unique gold D-O-R-S necklace. Diana was laid to rest just as she would have wanted, 'keeping the old end up' even in death.

Paradoxically in her last years that bleached mane came to represent something much more than a glamour image. Kept safe in an extraordinary way from the ravages of chemotherapy, it was as if it symbolised her indomitable will to overcome all forms of adversity and to demonstrate to all that, no matter what happens to you, life is always worth living and fighting for. She knew despair, heart-break, failure, immense wealth and terrifying poverty. She received adulation as a movie star and at times was booed in sleazy small room night clubs where drunks shouted 'Show us your tits'. But she came to understand that all these things were, equally, illusions – a belief which strengthened the courage in the face of adversity which she had always showed.

Admirers came to her funeral from all walks of life. Contrasting with the local priests and the bishop's representative was Charlie Kray, mourner himself and for his twin brothers, Ronnie and Reggie. There was Patrick Holt, who appeared in one

241

of her first films, and Richard O'Sullivan who was in one of her last. Diana's love was all-embracing, so all mingled together, all were welcome.

Out of diffidence the majority of locals stayed outside in the church grounds, where the service was relayed to them over loudspeakers. Those who went inside found themselves equally welcomed. The only part of the church cordoned off was to the left of the sanctuary. That was reserved for the press and the equipment and paraphernalia of television crews.

In the very centre of the sanctuary on trestles stood Diana's coffin. There was a large gold crucifix screwed to the top and a plaque which simply read: 'Diana Dors Lake. Aged 52 years.'

The church was filled with the perfume of flowers. There were innumerable, elaborate floral displays, in the shapes of hearts, crosses, stars, and round and square cushions, mostly in Diana's favourite colour, pink. A cross of white carnations and pink rosebuds from Alan and Jason stretched the length of the coffin. The card read:

'To my own sweet love. Only a whisper away. Love always.'

Beneath the trestles, single red roses in separate gold-sparkle dusted tubes were the tribute of Richard Dawson and sons Mark and Gary.

In the front pew, which the Sacred Heart community always left for their celebrity husband and wife, sat brokenhearted Alan holding tightly to his sister Vilma's hand, husband Ken, Jason and his grandfather. Alan had hoped that Mark and Gary would have been sitting there too. The actor had been expecting them to arrive ever since Diana's death. When at the last minute they phoned and told him they would not be coming over, Alan was shocked and upset:

"The boys said it would be too hard for them to bear, but it was the same for us all."

With the conclusion of the entry hymn 'Dear Lord and Father of mankind', Fr Fontanari addressed the congregation.

"This is above all a religious occasion calling for prayer from those who wish to pray, but requiring decorum from everyone out of respect for our sister Diana, and her sorrowing family."

From that moment Alan stemmed his tears and became composed. The Mass was full of the optimism and joy that comes from knowing that death is not the end but the beginning of life. Mixing with the themes of hope and expectancy came that of thanksgiving for a wonderful life and the great things God had done through Diana, even though all had hoped she could have lived longer. Bishop Westwood's was perhaps the best explanation:

"Why God takes a person who still has so much to give is of course the supreme human question.

"I believe we live in a fallen world. A world where things go desperately wrong. Where our best hopes will be dashed. I believe the whole purpose of faith is to help us to cope in a world where this sort of tragedy happens. What I would say about Diana is, all that we can do is to be extremely thankful for what she had. We must be grateful we had that much."

Actor Lionel Jeffries read the lesson, fittingly taken from 1 Corinthians 13, St Paul's great poem about love.

Patrick Holt had this to say:

"I'm here to wish 'au revoir' to our darling Diana, a lovely girl, with all the heart and love we can give her – an 'au revoir' because I know we shall meet again. She will always be with us.

Patrick Holt read a poem chosen by Alan, Scott Holland's 'Death is Nothing At All'. It was a remimer that Diana was not far away – in another room, if you like. "And just because she is out of sight do not let her be out of mind. Think of her, pray for her – she is somewhere very near."

Father Brian O'Sullivan, representing Bishop Cormac Murphy O'Connor, said something that a bishop rarely, if ever, says of an actress:

"She was truly sensational in every sense of the word, in

243

her faith, in her witnessing to that faith and in the way she faced death."

But perhaps everyone's view of Diana was best summed up in a postcard a lady had sent to Fr Fontanari which he held aloft and then read out:

"Dear Father, I am without faith. I know that something is missing in my life. Like millions, I loved our dear Diana, not as a sex goddess, but as a genuine person who one could feel would be-friend you as a warm human being.

"My heart is saddened and sympathy goes to their darling son. Without her lovely being, our world is much the poorer. I will now search for what she found."

At Communion, Fr Brian O'Sullivan spoke to the congregation:

"Will those wishing to receive Communion please go to Fr Fontanari and Fr Dominic – and those of you who cannot receive but would like a special blessing, will you come forward to me."

Alan's closest friend, Freddie Starr, who throughout the service stood with his wife Sandy beside Faith Brown, Anthea Redfern and her husband, and Shirley Bassey, without any hesitation at all moved toward the priest. First Freddie stood in front of Fr O'Sullivan with great dignity. Then he bowed his head for the blessing. Others followed him. Soprano soloist Wendy Kessack sang Handel's 'I know that my Redeemer liveth', and when most of the congregation had returned to their places, they joined in the singing of one of Diana's favourite hymns, 'Amazing Grace'.

For the final Commendation, Gluck's 'Dance of the Blessed Spirits' accompanied the pall-bearers as they came forward to lift Diana's coffin onto their shoulders. When they emerged from the church the people outside were huddled against the chill of an overcast May morning, their vigil ended. They solemnly watched while the coffin was led out of church by the small Italian priest and servers. As it was put in the hearse, Alan, with a fur lined brown suede coat covering his shoulders, looked at

Jason and the two joined hands clinging tightly to one another.

There was gasps of recognition from the crowd as stars and celebrities came up to Alan and then stood behind him, Jason and the family mourners. The hearse edged slowly forward. Only the revving of engines and the closing of doors could be heard as the funeral cortège formed, then picked its way carefully through the hundreds of people on its mile-long journey to Sunningdale cemetery. Here, there were yet more mourners, as well as another battery of photographers and film camermen, ready to frame forever in close-up these final emotional moments.

In the shade of the sycamore tree at the far end of the cemetery, Diana's coffin was gently lowered into the ground. A tiny crab apple tree which Alan and Jason had planted was already showing signs of blossom.

Once again drawing on his resources of strength and courage, for Diana numbered among his dearest friends, Fr Fontanari led the formal committal and farewell. The last part of the ritual was, however, reserved for Alan, and it was one which would appear on the covers of most of the 'dailies' next morning. He bent down and picked up a small pink rosebud from his own personal wreath, kissed it tenderly and then let it fall with care onto the newly laid coffin. It was his last and most poignant gesture of farewell.

23

STOP THE WORLD

Alan Lake returned to Orchard Manor, and while his guests were taking refreshment, he changed out of the pin-striped black suit he was wearing and took it to the garden. There, as if it were a continuation of the ritual, he set fire to the garments and burnt them to ashes.

The last occasion the actor had worn that particular suit also meant separation from his beloved Diana: he had been in the dock of Reading Assize Courts, having been charged with assault. This time the separation was for ever, and Alan Lake never wanted to see those particular items of clothing again.

Apart from the magnificent gold lamé dress with its matching full length cape in which he had had Diana clothed for burial, this was the only item of clothing Alan removed from the house. Everything else remained as it was.

Of the sackfuls of mail that kept arriving after her death, only a minimal number of letters were opened. The family explained:

"Alan had so much mail. Some of the letters were all about illness and cancer. These just served to drag him down."

The widower could not accept the fact that Diana was mortal as all human beings are. He still expected to see her in the house wearing one of her beautiful kaftans, busily preparing their meals or strolling round the magnificent gardens. Most of all he expected to see her engaged in her favourite occupation, swimming in their pool. And when he sat down on the cream brocade settee he waited for her to come in and sit beside him, to cuddle up and hear her husky voice saying "You're smoking too much, Lakey," when he reached for yet another cigarette.

In the immediate period following Diana's death, the

enormity of what had happened did not sink in. There was much
going on. Within days of the funeral he was away playing a
demanding role in an episode of television's 'Juliet Bravo'. Then
he played the part of an Irish artist in a Hammer House of Horror
episode. In between these he took over some of Diana's
engagements. He agreed to open a fête at Sheffield, near
Basingstoke, and when the actor knew it was for charity, did as his
wife would have, and waived the £1,000 fee.

One of Alan's immediate tasks was to design a fitting and
worthy memorial for his beloved wife. The local council rejected
the original plans, saying they were far to grandiose and ornate
and not in keeping with the other gravestones in the cemetery. In
the end Alan designed a headstone with Diana's and his favourite
flowers. A spray of daffodils were to be embossed onto pure white
marble. He also composed the wording:

Always Remembered
Diana Dors Lake
1931 – 1984
Forever Loved
'Only A Whisper Away'

The actor learnt too, that in Swindon Jim Masters was
endeavouring to have a worthy memorial for Diana in the form of a
full-sized statue placed in the Brunel Centre.

"I think it's important," said the Mayor, "that something
goes up in her memory. We have not produced many famous
people, and she was famous for being a tremendously good actress
and a good, loyal Swindonian."

In June and the early part of July Alan was almost always
away from home during the day. He took parts in 'The Gentle
Touch', 'Bergerac' and 'Lytton's Diary'. The actor hated leaving
Jason for any length of time, though there was usually someone at
Orchard Manor – the young valet, Rob, who lived in, or Mrs Webb
who came in some mornings during the week to attend to the

house. As often as not at weekends, instead of facing the loneliness of a home without its 'Lady', they went to friends at Brighton.

Jason was coping with the tragedy manfully. Like Alan, it had never really dawned on him that his mum would not pull through. She had taken two cancer operations in her stride; nothing seemed to daunt her. When Diana went into the Princess Margaret Hospital, young Jason was told that it was simply a small problem and that she would soon be well again. It came as a tremendous shock when Alan broke the news that this time she would not be coming out of hospital.

Jason had, in many ways, inherited his mother's strength and will-power. Although he was stunned, numb inside, he tried to keep up appearances for his father's sake. Young as he was, he knew the devastating effect Diana's death had had on Alan, and he did his best to ease the burden.

"How he's done it, I don't know," Alan told his friends. "He's so mature, so brave."

Alan desperately wanted to arrange a holiday for Jason, though not really in the mood for one himself. Knowing that he would be unable to cope with Marbella, in Spain, where Diana had planned for 'The Three Musketeers', he chose Greece. The reservations were made for father and son to go to Mykonos, where they would be assured some peace and quiet. The departure date was set for after Diana's Memorial Service.

When the idea of such a service was mooted for St Martin-in-the-Fields, the church customarily chosen by show business people for these occasions, Alan made a request for it to be held in a Catholic church. Mgr Leonard, Chaplain of the Catholic Stage Guild, was approached, and the venue fixed for Westminster Cathedral on July 24 at 12 noon.

The ceremony was held in the crypt of the Cathedral. Mgr Leonard and Fr Fontanari officiated in the presence of a small gathering of family and personal friends, including the authors and Violet Kirwan, who claims to be Diana's greatest fan. Unlike the glittering turn-out for Diana's funeral, only a small number of show business personalities turned up for her Memorial. Alan, somewhat disappointed, said simply:

"I suppose they are all busy working."

But for those who did attend he was grateful, and he said the same to each and every one:

"Bless you, and thank you so much for coming."

Alan tried really hard to keep cheerful as he and his fourteen-year-old son relaxed in Greece. It was not until afterwards, when they were waiting in the coach queue for the airport that he suddenly realised that when they arrived home, Diana would not be there. Then he broke down.

"I'm sorry, Jason. I'm gone." Tears poured from his eyes.

"That's alright dad." Jason put his arms round his father. "Don't worry about it."

Once back at Orchard Manor, Alan telephoned Violet Kirwan. He sounded depressed.

"It wasn't the same without Di," he told her. "Things were very trying at times. You see, darling, she was such a great cuddler . . . such a warm person, and had so much feeling in her. She was so wonderful, darling, and I bloody well miss her."

There was a pause, then he said, "God bless you, Violet, and pray hard for me." There were two more calls within the next couple of days. In both he was in a similarly low state.

On August 19, Alan and Jason were at Stringfellows night club to receive a cheque for the Imperial Cancer Research Fund. Next morning the newspapers carried a picture of the smiling pair, Alan holding a cheque in his hands. While most people seeing the photograph believed him to have picked up, he was, in reality, becoming more despondent. Bernie Winters said later, "He seemed very down. I told him to come and see me and to telephone me."

The following night he made his regular phone call to Violet.

"We spoke about Freddie Starr," Violet told us. "He said how he loved him, as if he were his very own brother. Then his voice became weary and he asked me why he was always cast as a baddie: those were the only parts he was ever offered. I told him that was because he played them so good. Then he thanked me for being so kind to him, said God bless, and put the phone down."

Alan was now beginning to lose interest in his work. Diana had been his inspiration and number one fan. She considered him an actor without par. But she was no longer there to share his success. He began to spend more time in the house, showing little enthusiasm for anything.

Ironically, Diana had spent some time talking about bereavement on Breakfast Television:

"When people lose someone, everyone rallies around for five minutes and then there is a fixed period of time when one is supposed to 'get over' a death. After that, people say, come on, you've had plenty of time to mourn, now get up and go, pull yourself together. But I think this is the time you need help most. At the beginning, when everyone's rallying round, you're also being carried along by nervous energy anyway, because of the shock of losing someone. It's months later when you come home to an empty house or you remember everyday things, that everyone else is gone."

How true these words became of her own husband. Friends did visit Orchard Manor, but they were more likely than not to ring him up to invite him to a party. Alan found excuses for refusing.

According to Jason, it was in September that his father's depression became markedly worse. Just after Diana had died Alan sensed her presence very strongly. He felt her beside him, and her perfume, 'Ma Griffe', which she had worn on the day they met, seemed to fill the air. In the drawing room the large oil painting of her looked down upon the settee where they had sat close together. Her cuddly toys were strewn on the bed just as she had left them, and the en-suite wardrobe was packed tight with her dresses and shoes.

After a while, though, Diana's presence was no longer so

253

tangible, and he began to look for her. He rushed frantically from room to room looking for her. In a frenzied effort to bring back his 'lover', he played videos of her, uninterrupted, for days at a time on the giant screen that dominated one end of the drawing room. Drawers where they kept their own personal memorabilia were emptied. It was all in vain.

When the truth that Diana was not coming back finally sank in, he began blaming God for taking away his wife. He became angry and bitter. He found it very difficult to accept what had happened to him, and churned away inside, as many of the bereaved do.

Further, he looked back on their life together and began to feel enormous guilt pangs about the dance he had led her. The days of alcohol addiction concerned him enormously now. He could have made life so much more pleasant for his wife. In his Bible, the one given him by Fr Fontanari which he read daily, the marker was left, finally, in Isaiah, Chapter 5, where the prophet speaks about the evils of drink.

The guilt pangs worsened. Everything now combined to send the tormented man on a downward spiral. He began experiencing again the darkness of soul which had afflicted him when Diana's cancer had re-occurred. Dr Lockston diagnosed manic depression, and advised hospitalisation with immediate medical treatment.

With deep depression came tiredness, inability to sleep, loss of appetite, and loss of confidence and self-esteem. A terrible feeling of inadequacy led him to turn down work and to avoid friends.

Being a non-drinking alcoholic made life far worse for Alan. All the pressures and frailties which had turned him to drink in the first place were still there: the old fears and inhibitions, lack of faith in himself, and an incapacity to cope. Neither had he lost the intense sensitivity which is part of the alcoholic's make-up and which makes him far more vulnerable to depression and self-pity when life turns against him.

Without anything else to minimise the pain, the guilt, the emptiness, Alan relied more than ever on drugs. But they did not work for him. It was proper medication he needed, the sort that only a hospital could provide. Now, however, there was no Diana to make him go.

Nobody really understood what was happening to Alan Lake, least of all young Jason, who was now the only person in the house. Alan's valet and cook, Rob, was no longer required, as the master of the house became more of a recluse. Because he was a good actor, he was also fully capable of camouflaging his real feelings. When Vilma and Ken visited Orchard Manor, which they frequently did, and when Cyril, his father, stayed with him for about six weeks after Diana's death, they had no idea what was going on in his mind. Neither after they left, did they detect anything in his voice during their regular telephone conversations.

In early September, when his sister rang to say they would be going on holiday in Venice, Alan said:

"Oh, Vil, please light a candle for me and Diana in St Mark's Basilica. Don't forget, will you. That's what Di and I did . . . we lit one to our love when we were there."

After promising to do as her brother asked, Vilma told us:

"We then made plans for Christmas, and we wanted Alan and Jason to come to us in Stoke-on-Trent. Alan readily agreed to this, and when we spoke of our son Mark's wedding in February of 1985, he straight away wrote it down in his diary and promised to be there, just as he and Diana had been for Glyn's wedding."

On September 11, Jason's fifteenth birthday, the authors spoke to Alan at Orchard Manor. Although it was a lovely warm evening he looked cold and tired. His face was gaunt and his eyes red, and he shivered, drawing hard on cigarette after cigarette.

"Jason is having a few of his friends in for a little celebration," he said, with an attempt at brightness.

But he seemed unsure of himself, absent-minded even. Then, as the subject inevitably turned to his wife, the tears which had gradually been filling his eyes suddenly overflowed and ran unchecked down his pallid cheeks, disappearing inside the neck of his T-shirt. He mentioned how worried he was about a three-part article on Diana and himself soon to be published in *TV Times*.

"The press," he said, "only write what they want to write...as they see it...they don't see love. Aah..." A great sigh seemed to come from the depths of his very being. "Our love. None of them know." He shook his head and his face crumpled. "Nobody understands. Oh, I'm, sorry...I'm gone."

When we left, Jason was comforting his father.

Evidently Alan could not prevent himself from losing interest in life. Even the good news that Jason had secured a part as a young Russian boy in Stephen Poliakoff's *Breaking the Silence* at London's Barbican Centre, did not, as proud as he was of his young son, cheer him as it would normally have done. He was now at the stage where he did not even want to speak to people. When the phone rang he would, as often as not, pretend it was the answering machine taking the call or that he himself was simply an employee who would take a message for Mr Lake. He seemed unable to cope with either the people in show-biz or the show-biz world.

Violet Kirwan continued to receive the regular calls, especially on Thursdays and Saturdays, his two worst days: Thursday, the day he and Diana met, and Saturday, the day they got married. He also had neighbours from across the way to sit with him and talk – Freddie Starr and his wife Sandy were at the ready to go to their friend's side to help him through the day or night.

"He started to lean on me more and more," said Freddie. "What began with long intimate talks ended with us walking down to the cemetery and sitting beside her grave. Alan would sit there and weep and lean his shoulder on me. I tried to comfort him, but then I got emotional and cried too. Then he would try and console me. As time went on the visits to the grave became more frequent. They were almost a ritual."

As the future began to look bleaker and the depression

deepened, Alan began to see death as a sweeter alternative.

"When he visited mum's grave early in the morning and late at night to avoid visitors and to be alone," said Jason, "dad just gazed and prayed that God would take him too."

Freddie Starr later revealed that Alan had admitted to taking a handful of pills in order to do away with himself – but had spat them out again:

"Alan was now telling me that he couldn't cope any more; that he didn't know how to carry on – I told him he had Jason to care for, and begged him to keep going. And again, when he phoned me in the middle of the night, hardly able to speak from grief, I said 'hold on, I'll be over,'"

But Alan was becoming more and more convinced that what he had contemplated doing was *not* wrong for him, and this attitude persisted as his condition deteriorated. Jason recalls:

"One night dad asked me if I'd be able to manage without him. He told me that he wanted to get off, to stop the world. He had had enough. I knew what he was saying alright, and it worried me deeply."

According to Freddie Starr, Alan began sensing the presence of his wife again: "He told me she was all around him. She was everywhere, but he was alone." The things she had said, the things they did, all came flooding back. The actor felt that she was coming for him. Poems that Diana had encouraged him to compose as a means of therapy saw daylight again. One dated back to his alcoholic days. In the period following Diana's operation the previous October, he had, while she lay sleeping, written:

> 'Sweet headed lady
>   my sugar baby doll,
> I'm as much for you
>   as a gangster is to a moll
> Remember the times
>   we laughed as well as cried.'

On Saturday September 22, Alan phoned Violet Kirwan
and read these lines to her:

> 'For I dream of us being
>   Forever side by side.
> How I ache my love
>   to hold you in my arms.
> Sweet headed woman
>   don't kill me with your charms.'

Violet remembers:

"Alan was so sad. He asked, did I know that it was soon the
anniversary of the day Di and he first met. I said I knew all of their
special dates. He then told me he missed her dearly, and could
smell her perfume and even cuddled the soft toys on their bed.
Then he said, 'What will become of me, Violet?'. By this time I
was in tears, but trying not to sound as if I was crying. He asked
me what was the matter. I said that I just had a tickle in my throat.
I asked Alan if he was doing any more work, but he didn't say. He
said that Jason was either getting work, or gone to work. I couldn't
understand him very well. Then he said there was someone at the
door and that he would ring me back."

He did so the next day.

"He apologised to me for the day before. 'I hope I didn't
upset you,' he said.

"'You could never upset me, Alan, you're too kind to hurt
any one.'

"'Oh, darling, you don't know how much it hurts. I'm so
lonely. I keep seeing Di wherever I look. She won't leave me. She
doesn't know how much I need and miss her. Why is it when you
love someone so much, you lose them?'"

"I tried to comfort him. I reminded him of what Di said,
that if it wasn't her who was suffering, it would be some other poor
soul. He seemed to agree. I told him he was very welcome to ring
any day or night. He said, 'Thank you', and that he loved me for

my kindness. I was by this time crying, as he sounded so sad and distant."

Thursday September 27 brought a surprise phone call from Alan in reply to Violet's regular weekly letters. He seemed a little more cheerful but did not talk to her for long, saying he had a lot of people in the house. This was not the case. Alan was in fact by himself.

The following evening, September 28, Charlie Kray visited Orchard Manor and had dinner with Alan.

"He was rather down and depressed," Charlie subsequently revealed, "and he wasn't interested in the food."

Alan did not make his accustomed call to Violet on Saturday September 29. In her diary she made this note:

"I don't know why Alan's not phoned me today, he always does..."

Sunday, September 30, there was still no news from Orchard manor. As it transpired Alan and Jason had gone to Brighton. Violet was to hear that in a bid to escape his torment he had passed the weekend high on drugs. Unaware of this, Mrs Kirwan telephoned Fr Fontanari; Diana's 'little Italian priest' had recently returned from his vacation in Italy. Fr Fontanari told Violet that he had seen Alan in the village a few days before.

"He looked very strange," said the priest, "his eyes were very glazed and he just stared in front of him. I said, 'Alan, what can I do to help you. You look so pale and thin. Let me help you if I can, won't you?'

"No, Father, it's nice of you, but there's nothing you can do, – thanks for asking.' Then Alan just walked on . . . he seems so lost . . . what can I do for him, Violet? I talk to him, but he doesn't seem to hear me."

Alan did in fact have an appointment with Fr Fontanari during that coming week, but he did not keep it. The priest remembers bumping into his friend in the village on a later day.

"Poor Alan. He was in a very, very bad way. He told me that Jason was due to start rehearsals in a few days. He was pleased, but also said he was concerned about his son's O levels – that he wasn't studying enough for them. He was so depressed."

In his increased dementia Alan told those close to him that Diana was talking to him all the time, trying to sort out his problems. So as not to forget her words, Alan would speak them into a tape recorder. When his son asked him what he was doing, Alan answered, "It's alright, your mother is telling me what to do."

Somewhere around this period, the suffering actor had written:

> 'I am holding back the tears,
>   being strengthened by my fears.
> Your home-spun philosophies
>   are like mirrors in the trees.
> I feel like My Lord,
>   being nailed up to a tree.
> Let me be.
>   Let me be.
>   Let me be.'

On Friday October 5, Violet received a letter from Alan with the large photograph of his wife which he had promised her.

Next day Alan was due to go to the christening of Freddie Starr's two children, but he phoned to say that Jason had flu and that he wanted to stay with him.

"Then he confessed," says Freddie "that the depression had got too bad, and he hadn't wanted to spoil the occasion for me.

"Alan did come to my home that night, though. It was about 6 o'clock. By then the christening was over and everyone had gone. He looked terrible. His face was drawn and he looked so thin. We sat down in the lounge drinking coffee. He said he just didn't know how to carry on.

"I tried to cheer him up. We hatched a plan. I told him he should sell his house, and we'd open a pub together – but he seemed unable to look to the future. He said he wanted to end it all. So I tried to shock him out of it.

"At 10 o'clock Alan got up to leave. He had been with me for four hours. We walked down the drive to his car. Then he embraced me and said, 'Frieddie, I love you very much. I love you second only to Diana and Jason.'

"After that he walked through the garden gate and drove off."

It had been an extremely bad day for Alan Lake – one where he had paced the house, talked into the tape recorder, was frightened, and hardly recognised Jason. After his time with Freddie, there can be little doubt that the day's pattern continued throughout the night.

On top of everything else, on Sunday he smashed his white Cadillac, Diana's favourite car, which he knew would have upset her.

On Monday October 8, Alan spoke to Max Clifford, Freddie Starr's publicity man, who had also worked for Diana. He said:

"I don't think I can go on any longer."

That evening, later than usual, Alan went round to the Sacred Heart Church to pray. It was about 8 o'clock and the door had been locked for the night. Father Anthony, one of the priests of the community, opened it for him, saw him into the little church, and, feeling that the actor wanted to be in there by himself, returned to the house.

The next morning, Tuesday October 9, Alan phoned impressario Paul Raymond, saying that he wanted to arrange a belated birthday party for Jason.

"He said he wanted to celebrate it at my Night Club, La Vie en Rose," recalls Mr Raymond, "but the more he chatted, the more I realised that the birthday party was just a front. The truth was that he was trying to force himself out of his grief."

Alan Lake's agent for over 20 years, Peter Green, spoke to the actor that day too:

"I just knew he was grieving. He was subdued. He phoned to say he wanted work as a way of forgetting."

October 10 dawned, the day he and Diana had first met, sixteen years to the day, and the memory of it was as sharp as a flashing neon light. Alan had dreaded the anniversary this year. Waking up after a fitful sleep, alone in their king-sized bed, was always the worst time in Alan Lake's day; it was then that the awesome truth would hit him. Every day was the same – destroyed before it had begun. It had been like this for the past five months. Nothing had helped. Not sleeping pills, not drugs, not even his prayers and constant visits to the church and to Diana's grave.

On his bedside table he kept his prayer cards. One was a prayer for peace and rest by Cardinal Newman:

'May He support us
all day long,
till the shades lengthen
and the evening comes,
and the busy world is
hushed, and the fever
of life is over, and
our work is done.
Then in His mercy
may he give us a safe lodging,
and a holy rest
and peace at the last.'

The other was Minnie Louise Haskins' famous verses about trust in God:

'I said to the man who stood at the gate of the year:
Give me a light that I may tread more safely into the unknown.
And he replied, Go out into the darkness and put your hand
    in the hand of God.
That shall be to you better than light and safer than a known
    way.'

In the state of turmoil he was in, it seems that Alan found his own meaning in these verses. He hoped that by going out into the darkness he would not only find the hand of God but his wife's too.

Diana was tantalisingly everywhere but at the same time not there. The bedroom was a froth of pink nylon and organdie. The ceiling, a canopy of gossamer, complemented the magnificent crystal chandelier, falling from its centre. Everything was just as Diana had left it. The same bed from which, during the last days of her life, he had gently lifted his beloved wife, carried the slight little body – then no more than eight stone in weight – through ankle-deep carpet to the bath, pink like the bedroom, kidney-shaped and large enough for two, with carpeted steps leading up to it. On the dressing table, kidney-shaped too, stood her perfume, nail varnish, make up – exactly as she had left it the day she went into hospital for the last time.

But the house was now on the market, and today, of all days, there would be people coming to view it. Of late, Alan had hardly bothered to dress up; as often as not his pink bathrobe saw him through the morning and after that he changed to jeans and T-shirt. But on this day he was his usual meticulous self. He bathed, dressed up and then drove Jason to South Ascot railway station to catch the train to London. Having kissed Jason goodbye, Alan returned to Orchard Manor.

"He was a little more cheerful after putting Jason on the train," says Mrs Webb, the housekeeper, "but then he became depressed again, remembering it was the anniversary of his and Mrs Lake's first meeting. I told him to cheer up and reminded him that there was someone coming to look at the house."

Because he was so pale, the housekeeper suggested he put some rouge on his face. But Alan ignored this suggestion and went up to his study, where he spent the rest of the morning writing. He did not emerge until just before lunch.

At 1 o'clock, Alan took a phone call. It was journalist Jean Rook, who had heard that Orchard Manor was on the market and wanted to talk to him about it. He said to her:

"I'm sorry. I'm in a bit of a state. It's a bad day today, a very bad day. It's the day I met her."

Later he added:

"Everything's going on here today. It's bedlam here today."

Miss Rook sympathised and apologised for bothering him at such a bad time, arranging to telephone him again on Monday. His final words to her were:

"Goodbye, Rookie darling. Goodbye."

After this, according to Honor Webb, Alan went around switching on all the lights in the house and the swimming pool. He took a second telephone call, she said, and afterwards sat at the bottom of the stairs with his head in his hands.

"I can't go on," he said to her. "I've got such big problems. I'm in more trouble than you'll ever know."

Alan also told his housekeeper yet again that he could not live without Diana. He then went upstairs and Mrs Webb returned to the kitchen. Minutes later she heard a bang.

"I rushed up, thinking he had pulled something down over himself. He wasn't in his study or bedroom, so I poked my head in Jason's bedroom. I couldn't see him, so I came out again and went in another door to the lad's bathroom. Through the adjoining door of the suite I could then see Mr Lake, lying curled up on the floor at the foot of Jason's bed. A single-barrelled shot-gun was beside him. It was then I could see he'd blown his brains out."

Only the golden snake on the black walls witnessed what had happened. Alan left no note. He did not need to. Believing he would meet again the woman he could not live without gave him the nerve he needed to tread into the unknown. Written on the same grey lined writing pad he always used for his verses, were the last lines he ever wrote, maybe that very morning:

'Tick tock
Clock on the wall,
I believed in our love,
Yes – I believed it all.'

24

COULD WE HAVE DONE MORE?

The belief that Alan was reunited with Diana sustained the congregation of over 150 friends and relatives who attended the funeral of Alan Lake, as it must have done Jason, though this was a thinner, paler and less boyish-looking young man than the one who had attended his mother's funeral. Sorrow had made him grow up very quickly.

For the service Jason stood, sat and knelt, with his head held high and his back straight, occupying the place his father had done five months before. The card on his wreath, placed on his father's coffin, read simply, 'God Bless you Daddy. Love Jason.' Aunt Vilma squeezed his hand resolutely. Any tears Jason shed were shed in the privacy of his own room.

Father Fontanari looked inconsolable as he proceeded on to the sanctuary with Fr Anthony to celebrate the Requiem Mass. Just before Fr O'Sullivan rose to give his address, Freddie Starr arrived. It had been a rush for him. He had boarded an aeroplane in Ireland that very morning, where he had been touring. He stood at the back, looking neither to left nor right. Bewilderment showed on a pale face. Like so many others, he asked, why did he do it?

It was in an endeavour to answer that question that Alan's parish priest began by reading a statement sent him by the Lakes' physician Dr Lockston:

'Alan was recovering from a nervous breakdown earlier this year when Diana became mortally ill. During the last few weeks of her life, he hardly ever left her side and in the last few days hardly every slept. Immediately after her death he was called upon to organise a very public funeral. Due to physical exhaustion caused by these events the depression returned.'

Father O'Sullivan went on to say that no one can presume to anticipate the Coroner's verdict, "but I think it was pretty obvious that what happened to Alan in that last tragic moment of his life was not what Alan, had he been himself, would have done. Because we know, for instance, that over the last few months since Diana's death, Alan came to the church many times on his own to pray. And that is not the act of someone who is in total despair.

"And yet, though he was able to come and pray, nevertheless the black darkness of despair was building up inside his mind. We know when these things happen people are not themselves, and the verdict of the Coroner's Court normally is, 'suicide while the balance of the mind was disturbed.'"

This was, in fact, the result of the inquest held at Chertsey on November 16. Dr Lockston reported that the actor had been diagnosed as suffering from manic depression, possibly complicated by drug abuse. Verdict: he killed himself while suffering from a depressive illness.

"As we face the tragedy of the reality of this service this morning," Fr O'Sullivan continued, "we look back to the triumphant funeral of Diana, and we can understand something of the terrible loss that Alan experienced and how empty his life must have seemed since she went. The scriptures of the Church show us that agony of the mind is not just a modern phenomenon. The reading from the book of Lamentation, which we have just heard, is a cry of a man in the darkness of depression. And what is even more striking, is that in the gospel, like him, Jesus himself on the cross cries out, 'My God, My God . . . why have You forsaken me?'"

Alan had compared his suffering to that of Jesus being nailed to a tree, and he had also felt the desolation of being abandoned by God. So indeed had Diana at one stage of her mortal illness. She had told Fr Fontanari that on Good Friday, the words of Jesus from the cross, 'I thirst, I thirst', kept reverberating in her mind.

Father O'Sullivan offered no answer to this terrible

physical and spiritual pain, save that in Jesus, God himself experienced the human condition:

"The one who cried from the cross, 'My God, My God, why have You forsaken me', was the one who three days later was raised to life again by His Father. So by taking upon himself our pain, our grief, our anguish, our degradation, he rose to offer us a new life – a promise that no matter how dark our life may be in this world there is still a greater life yet to come, a life in which all our deepest wishes, our deepest longings, will be fulfilled.

"Jesus offers us a solution to our desolation and depression, and that is a relationship that can never let us down. A relationship which will endure into eternity because God is our Father. He's Alan's Father. He called Alan to Himself in a tragic way. But it is to a home He has called him, to a home where the ever-loving Father is the one who understands and who forgives.

"Our prayer is that Alan has found Diana, because all love is given by God. Although human death interrupts our loving relationships, the love itself endures beyond the grave. So today our prayer is that Alan and Diana are reunited in their love for one another, and now open to the infinite love and joy of God's love."

In his sermon Fr O'Sullivan asked the great question – "We all share a common sense of grief. Could we have done more? Did we let him die? This is the very real tragedy."

There was certainly nothing anyone could have done once Alan's depressive illness returned, apart from seeking medical help for him. He could not have been convinced by argument, persuasion or even the love of Jason to continue living. Alan and Diana were soul mates. One could not function without the other. They could not bear to be apart.

Honor Webb saw it all:

"They were helplessly in love. And they never missed an opportunity to show it. Even if one of them had been out for a couple of hours, when they returned they greeted each other as if they'd been apart for a lifetime. Every inch of the house was filled with their love."

Freddie Starr also understood their love:

"No one can describe the love he had for Di. She was a real part of him. When she went he was just half a man."

Vilma and Ken knew and understood, and so did Jason. He said:

"Afterwards I understood why he couldn't get through the next few weeks. First, there was the anniversary of the day they met. Then it would have been mum's birthday, then dad's, and then their wedding anniversary, and then Christmas. He couldn't face all that."

'Love is a long time coming, my love, like Christmas to a child' were the opening words of one of Alan's poems. The actor was twenty-eight years old when he fell in love, but love was a longer time coming for Diana. They recognised it at first sight. Three days after they met, Alan proposed. "She accepted," he said, "and we both gave a sigh of relief that we had met *the one* at last."

Diana was able to camouflage the intensity of their relationship more easily than Alan. Being the stronger of the two there is no doubt that she could have survived if something had happened to Alan first. Even though her heart might be broken, Diana would have come through grief, refined and better able to give more. She *would* have had her religious programme.

Alan was not built that way. He wore his heart on his sleeve. His love for Diana was plain for all to see. The actor would have existed as a rudderless ship, which would have eventually floundered on the rocks. As it was, he made a tremendous effort after Diana's death. He took work on and, as Dr Lockston pointed out, arranged a very public funeral. He helped to tie up Diana's affairs, designed a very fitting and worthy headstone for her grave, and organised a memorial service. He also continued to act as a father to Jason and to help him over those initial months of loneliness. It was a superhuman effort because, although his heart was beating, he was already dead inside.

Alan would have died of a broken heart if he had not taken

his own life. This is the opinion that the authors formed of him. We knew he was literally pining away. Every time we mentioned Diana's name, tears came to his eyes. We also knew that he was neither eating, nor taking care of himself. The trouble was that there was no one around who the authority to say, "Alan, you've got to have treatment – see your doctor."

Many people expected Alan Lake to go back on the drink following his wife's death. They did not understand him. They did not understand love.

Neither would Alan ever have gone with another woman. He had said, "You only get lucky enough to enjoy something we had once in a lifetime. So I know I'll never have any relationship with a woman again – and that includes a physical relationship."

On the first anniversary of Mrs Lake's death, certain people decided to mark the occasion with a smear campaign in the national dailies. Michael Caborn-Waterfield, who over all the years had remained friends and business associates of both Diana and Alan, wrote an article in the *Daily Star* on May 7 1985, in which he accused both Alan and Diana of having affairs. He said that during Diana's illness, when Alan flew back from Athens to be at her bedside, he afterwards rushed straight into the arms of a girlfriend. And later, when Alan returned to Greece, he had, claimed Mr Caborn-Waterfield, "a torrid love affair" with a girl named Frances.

Were these the actions of a man so desperate to get to the bedside of his wife that, when all flights to London were fully booked, he was prepared to ask the American Air Force to allow him to travel with them and to parachute onto Salisbury Plain? Alan reached the hospital on the evening of September 3. He was with his wife all of the next day, leaving her only to catch an aeroplane back to Greece so that he could rush through his 'takes'. Alan was back in England on September 7, having finished his work in the 'Hart to Hart' episode. There was hardly time for a 'torrid love affair'.

Alan, it was also alleged in the article, was found by Diana in bed with their housekeeper, and had sex with another employee called 'Pixie'. Vernon Lovejoy, Diana's chauffeur, in an interview for the *News of the World*, May 12, also mentioned the girl, whom he described as a young drifter, whom Diana took on to help in the house for a short time. Lovejoy said that 'Pixie' would plait Alan's hair and paint his toe-nails, and that they were having sex.

David Bromfield of the *Mirror*, writing at the time of Alan's death, said he first met Alan Lake in September 1983 at Orchard Manor at 4 o'clock in the morning. Alan wanted him to meet British heavy-weight boxing champion David Pearce.

"While I was there a teenage girl helped Alan undress, shower and towel dry. She smothered him in powder and toilet water, painted his toe-nails silver and helped dress him."

No doubt the girl was the same one mentioned by Caborn-Waterfield and Lovejoy. But unlike them, Mr Bromfield, though bemused by Alan Lake's behaviour, never considered it to be a 'sex thing', a matter of him being unfaithful to his wife. In fact, the reporter quoted Alan as saying that he never had affairs, and that "having another woman just for physical pleasure seemed pointless".

When Pixie was in the Lakes' employ in September/October 1983, as general help around the house, Alan was in the throes of manic depression. After Diana's second operation he was unable to sleep for nights on end. He invariably made for the swimming pool area, where the showers and jacuzzi were located, in an effort to try to relax, often while his wife slept upstairs. No longer shy about his own body, having made *Playbirds* and *The David Galaxy Affair*, he thought nothing of going into the jacuzzi naked, whether in company or not. Diana knew all of her husband's idiosyncracies. Some years earlier, in her poem of love, 'What is A Lake', she had written:

'A Lake is a child-man – who likes you to bathe and dry him, wash his hair, and spoil him endlessly.'

There was hardly a woman who met Alan who did not find him attractive, fall for him even, and, as his sister admitted:

"He used to flirt with them all, but there was nothing in it. He always knew where to draw the line."

Violet Kirwan, well known in Brighton as the promoter of Diana's and Alan's Appreciation and Fan Club, received a photograph through the post on the anniversary of Diana's death. It was of Alan naked with a girl. A cover note read:

'Now see what you think of him'

This upset Violet greatly, until she realised on closer scrutiny that it was not a recent picture of Alan at all. His short cut hair dated him to the days of his sex-romp films, of which this was a still!

But the 'hate campaign' had not ended yet. About the same time Violet received a phone call:

"I've a video of him and Jason frolicking with young girls ..."

The caller said it was taken ten days before Alan's death, which would indeed correspond with his spending a weekend at Brighton, the same weekend he had resorted to heavy drugs to help him cope.

Not satisfied with maligning Alan, Caborn-Waterfield later turned on Diana. He said that when her sylph-like figure returned following the X-cel diet, she celebrated by having a year-long affair with a married man who happened to live close by.

It is common knowledge that Diana died just some six months after her slim-in on TVAM. She was far from well and on cancer-control tablets which made her violently sick. She had an enormous work load as an 'Agony Aunt', which she took very seriously. Then there was the film *Steaming*, as well as her son, husband and the house to look after.

Honor Webb contributed to an article in *Woman's Own* on April 13 1985, almost totally devoted to the remarkable love each had for the other. On May 7, two days after Diana's anniversary, she gave a contradictory interview to *The Sun* in which she said Diana had a secret lover with whom she planned to run away, and then start divorce proceedings. Alan too, she said, tried to seduce her. Both articles appeared on the same day, full of inconsistencies.

One of the great heartaches Alan experienced in the last months of his life with Diana, and known at that time to only a handful of people, was that he could not express his deepest possible love for her; she was too ill for sex. He cried when he spoke about it in private, and with utmost conviction he repeated:

"I shall never be unfaithful to my wife – even though she told me that I had a free hand to have affairs if I felt the need. But I turned down her offer – just as she had mine when I said similar words to her after my horse-riding accident. There would be no love pact for us."

In the last year of his own life, Alan wrote:

"So many marriages break down because couples don't work at them. You think – if only they had tried a little bit harder. It's worth the effort.

"People don't really take the marriage vows seriously. It's like the Lord's Prayer, which is learned at school. It's very sad that people don't really know what they are saying any more.

"If people are going to get married, then they should have a good think about the vows. After all, the words aren't there just to be read over you, they are there to help you.

"Take 'in sickness and in health', for example. You can't just leave that person aside because he or she is ill."

Diana, who was living on a knife edge since cancer struck in 1982, said many a time, "I don't know if I'm living or if I'm dying." It is very unlikely that a person of her maturity, responsibility and religious fervour would jeopardise eternity on one last fling.

Alan Lake had spent all his married life proclaiming to the world his love for Diana Dors. It was not until he took his own life that people believed him – and it is sad that even then, there were some who would not.

Love is sent from above

True love comes but once in your life,
And that's the one you make your wife,
So laugh at me yesterday's fool,
I'm nobody's tool as she walks through my brain and my heart.
She still shares my bed, shares my life and my load;
Like a stick to my drum, she's my children's sweet Mum,
Yes, the love of my life is still my wife;
My one true love, *was* sent from above,
She's my darling, my heartbeat, my love – X

Alan Lake

25

LOVE'S LAST GIFT – REMEMBRANCE

It was at the moment when his father's coffin was lowered into the grave at Sunningdale cemetery that Jason decided he wanted to be a star, to go to Hollywood to try to make a name for himself, so that his parents would be proud of him.

The first step of that quest was to perform at the Barbican. It was there, some hours after saying goodbye to his father at Sunningdale station, that two police officers had gently broken the news of Alan's death. Acting in *Breaking the Silence* did, however, have the effect of taking Jason's mind off his terrible ordeal. Further, the cast showed their sympathy and understanding at every turn. The young man performed admirably.

"I really enjoyed the play and the rest of the cast were a great bunch. I wasn't at all nervous – I just went out there and did my bit. And we had a full house almost every night."

When Jason left the Royal Shakespeare Company he returned to Sunningdale and stayed with the Blackburn family, close friends of Diana's. At Christmas he kept his date with uncle, aunt and grandfather at Stoke-on-Trent. Vilma said:

"He was lovely. He was fine. You know, what with Ken and our two boys Glyn and Mark around him, it was as if he had three dads looking after him."

On December 27 1984, they drove Jason to Heathrow airport to start a new life in America with step-brother, Gary Dawson. Diana and Alan, in a will made during Gary's years in England with them, stipulated that in the event of their deaths, Gary should be Jason's guardian, until the latter reached eighteen.

Gary was pleased with his appointment as legal guardian,

and so was Jason. The young American told the press:

"I regard Jason as my little brother. I've been appointed his legal guardian, which means I've got to be a dad to him as well now.

"Jason has very serious ambitions about becoming an actor. I shall introduce him to all my contacts in the Hollywood world of television and films.

"Even though I'm only seven years older than Jason, I feel I am in a position to look after him."

Vilma and Ken were more than satisfied.

"We feel very happy about Jason. We don't feel that we've lost him . . . in fact we've gained Gary! They speak to us every week on the phone, and Gary, well, he asks Ken's advice about everything.

"He's taken his new role as guardian very seriously. He's got Jason going to High School to finish off his education. This is what his daddy dearly wanted. He'll be pleased and so will Diana!"

The Thursfields were not sure why Mark was left out of the will. The press mentioned that Diana never forgot the bitterness shown to her by her eldest son; he blamed her for the break-up of the marriage to his father. For this he had never really forgiven her, and he rarely kept in touch.

A more delicate task for Ken and Vilma was to attend to the headstone for Alan's grave. There was never any doubt in their minds that it should match the beautiful one already designed by Alan for Diana, which was still waiting for the ground at the grave to settle before being put into place. Thus it too would be of simple white marble embossed with a spray of daffodils and gold lettering. After careful thought they decided on the wording:

Love's Last Gift
Remembrance
Alan Lake
1940 – 1984
Together Forever
'Only a Whisper Away'

Plans to erect a statue in memory of Diana in Swindon eventually fell through. There were those who thought an annual scholarship awarded to the town's most promising young actor would be a better idea. Money was the problem. Mr Hodson, Director of Arts and Recreation for Thamesdown Borough Coucil, said that the town was very much *for* Diana, but the small nucleus in favour of such a burse were not able to to raise the money for it. The council themselves could not. "Some said if you do it for one, then it means you have to do the same for others," Mr Hodson told the authors.

Orchard Manor and effects took six months to sell. In a will published on June 8 1985, the residue of the estate came to £208,000 after tax, solicitors' fees and maintenance. The fact that there was little else in the bank reflected the Hollywood life-style Diana had wished to maintain to the last.

The biggest surprise was the £132,702 that Alan Lake left to Jason and Gary. This was his own money, and it was certainly a rebuke to those who had written the actor off as someone who sponged off Diana.

Many fans come to Sunningdale cemetery. They come because of the woman Diana was. Now, both her own and her husband's headstones are in place, and there are always fresh floral tributes on both. Each time the authors go, there is always evidence of recent visitors. Sometimes a fan, or a family of fans even, are to be found arranging flowers, or sitting in silence on the bench beside the graves. No doubt they are hoping, praying – believing that two people with so much love to give are now together in a world where there will be no more partings, no more tears. As it is, they lie together in a quiet corner of a country cemetery, side by side – indeed, *only a whisper away*.

INDEX